F★CKBOY

A MEMOIR

Blake Jerome Humphreys

Printed in the United States of America.

Paperback ISBN: 979-8-9951340-0-8

Hardcover ISBN: 979-8-9951340-1-5

Ebook ISBN: 979-8-9951340-2-2

First Edition

Contents

For Kadyn and Karder. I love you more than anything.

THIS IS A
TRUE STORY.
Not inspired by real events.
Not loosely based on a life.
This happened.

"Hell is empty and all the devils are here."

– William Shakespeare

PROLOGUE

You don't want to read this.

Not because it's shocking.

Because it's familiar.

This is what happens when nobody tells you no. When attention feels like oxygen. When freedom looks

like movement and destruction feels like momentum.

I didn't fall apart. I accelerated.

I learned how to be wanted without being known. How to leave without leaving. How to turn desire into

noise, so I didn't have to listen to myself think.

People called it confidence.

People called it charm.

People called it a phase.

They were wrong.

This isn't a lesson.

This isn't an apology.

This is the damage, written exactly where it landed.

If you're looking for growth, stop here.

If you're looking for comfort, this isn't it.

But if you've ever confused chaos for freedom,

you're already in too deep.

Turn the page.

I

ALMOST FAMOUS

LIFE STARTS BEFORE YOU understand where you are, and it ends before you ever really do. This is mine. I grew up in Los Angeles, a semi-nepo baby before I even knew what that meant. Fame wasn't something we chased. It was just in the air, like smog. Normalized. Background noise. My grandparents were famous dancers. Hundreds of movies between them. Their names rolled in end credits long before I could read. My mother, Micky, followed that path halfway, recognizable but not untouchable. She appeared in films and television shows that people still reference casually, the way you mention an old song you forgot you loved. Micky grew up in the industry as a model. An actress. She was small-framed and beautiful. She had brown hair and an elegance about her. Her face could have been on the cover of Vogue, and it probably was at one point. Everywhere she went, men and women would stare at her. When she walked into a room, everything would stop and only start again when she allowed it to. She had presence, and she knew it. All of my looks I get from her. My grandmother, Jennifer, spent most of her life standing in for Elizabeth Taylor. Same silhouette. Same elegance. She moved through Hollywood without ever fully belonging to it, close enough to touch glamour, distant enough to survive it. I grew up on tennis courts. My grandfather, Jameson, was a well-known tennis coach, the kind who didn't just train athletes but also collected stories. He spent his time at the Playboy Mansion, then came home and taught discipline, repetition, and control. Glamour on one side of the gate. Routine, on the other hand. As a kid, I met celebrities the way other kids met their parents' coworkers. I didn't understand their significance. They were just adults with confident voices and expensive smiles. I spent a lot of my childhood at Jameson's house in the Hollywood Hills, a house with big, quiet rooms overlooking a city that never stopped performing. From the outside, it looked like privilege. From the inside, it felt like proximity without protection. I learned early that being close to greatness doesn't mean you're guided by it. It just means you see how empty applause can sound when it echoes down hallways no one actually lives in. I didn't know it then, but that environment taught me two things that would shape my life. How to perform and how to disappear.

Growing up, I had no social skills. I didn't learn how to read rooms or people because I was never allowed in either. I was homeschooled, isolated in a way that felt less like protection and more like containment. The world existed somewhere outside our walls, but it wasn't for us. It was dangerous. Corrupt. Watching. My mother, Micky, was deeply religious. That phrase doesn't quite cover it, but it's the closest polite language offers. Religion wasn't guidance in our house; it was law. It was fear with scripture attached. I wasn't allowed to eat at the table. I ate on the floor, sitting cross-legged, my food placed on paper bags like offerings. Sitting there, I was wondering why I wasn't good enough to sit at the table. No sugar. Ever. Pleasure was suspect. Enjoyment needed justification. Anything sweet was treated like a moral failure waiting to happen. Rules were absolute, and explanations were unnecessary. If I spoke out of turn, mispronounced a word, or questioned anything, anything at all, I was beaten. Not corrected. Not disciplined. Beaten. Ruthlessly. A heavy wooden loofah was nearby. A plastic hanger when it wasn't. The punishment was never about the mistake. It was about submission.

I still dream about the screaming.

Not hers. Mine. That sound stays with you. It settles somewhere deep, in the part of your nervous system that never quite learns what safety feels like. Even now, years later, my body remembers before my mind does. Loud noises. Sudden movements. The way my chest tightens when someone raises their voice, even in laughter. Makes me flinch, makes me feel not safe, like my childhood should have delivered but never did. To say Micky was religious is an understatement. God wasn't a source of comfort in our home. He was a witness. Always watching. Always disappointed. Used to justify cruelty and call it love. Used to turn obedience into virtue and fear into faith. I learned early that silence was survival. That compliance could pass for goodness. That pain, if endured quietly enough, was somehow holy. Those lessons didn't stay in childhood. They followed me into adulthood, into relationships, into the way I learned to disappear inside my own body. Into the way I confused control with care, intensity with intimacy, and chaos with love. I didn't know it yet, but the damage was already done. Everything that came later, fame, sex, drugs, running, was just me trying to outpace a childhood that never really ended. After so many brushes with death, this was just the first one. It began one quiet evening just like every other one. I was eight years old. I went with Micky to Jameson's house just like so many nights before. He lived high above the city. Several Mercedes-Benzes sat in the driveway. A Corvette slept in the garage. The house itself was massive, with five bedrooms, perched on a cliff overlooking the hills. There was a big pool out back. It was my favorite place to be growing up. It was 1994. That night, we slept in one of the guest rooms. Someone else had already taken the spare bed, and my grandfather told me to sleep on the floor under the wardrobe by the door. It was enormous, solid wood and glass, filled with knick-knacks and heavy decorations. It had to weigh close to a thousand pounds. I remember saying no. I chose to sleep on the floor between the two twin beds where Micky and her friend were sleeping. I woke up in the middle of the night, flying into the air. Up and down. Up and down. I did not know I was in an earthquake. I thought I was dreaming. Everything around me was crashing. Glass exploding. Furniture slamming. I heard Micky scream. I heard Jameson scream from the other room. Then it stopped. The wardrobe had fallen. Right onto the place where I was supposed to sleep. There was glass everywhere. Thousands of pieces. If I had listened, I would have died. That night was the Northridge earthquake of 1994. It measured 6.7. Little did I know this was just the first time I would almost meet death. The next morning, the house looked like it had been bombed. Furniture was overturned. The television lay face down on the floor. Glass covered every surface. I woke up wanting to watch Power Rangers, as nothing had happened. The TV wouldn't turn on. There was no power. I could hear sirens in the distance that never stopped. We could not drive anywhere. The roads were split and broken. The air felt heavy, wrong, like the city itself was holding its breath. That was one of the first times I experienced real chaos. Not fear. Chaos. The kind that arrives without warning and leaves nothing where it was. The kind that does not explain itself or apologize. That feeling stayed with me. As I grew, I watched Jameson move through the world untouched by it. He was rich. High status. Good looking. Tall. Composed. Hugh Hefner was his friend. Tony Bennett was his best friend. His phone calls were always coming from somewhere far away. New York. China. Wimbledon. "Sorry, can't make it, have to go to Bruce Willis's birthday party." On New Year's Eve every year, he went to the Playboy Mansion. I overheard him one time explicitly explaining an orgy he had been to in "The Grotto." Micky spent a lot of time there, too. Sitting by the pool collecting sun at every pool party as if she belonged. Jameson always had women around him, a lot of women. Young. Beautiful. Impossibly Asian, mostly. They moved through the house like proof of power and freedom. He was everything I thought survival looked like. Money. Fame. Style. Control. That was who I wanted to be. Chaos would follow me, but I welcomed it. Jameson taught me to embrace it. I never really had a father.

My biological father, John, and my mother separated when I was very young. Too young to remember anything of substance. Whatever memories I have of him feel like dreams. Fragmented. Unreal. Faces without weight—moments without sound. Everything I knew about him came from Micky. She told me he was a monster. A psycho. That he stalked her. That he hit her in the stomach while she was pregnant with me. She described him as dangerous, unstable, someone I should fear and never look for. I believed her. I had no other version of the story. So I grew up without a father. Not absent. Removed. Erased before I could ask questions. After the earthquake, my mother worked constantly. She was a nurse at a mental hospital and always picking up shifts. Always gone. I was a terror to all babysitters. Not difficult. Not mischievous. A full-scale psychological operation. Micky eventually stopped hiring individual nannies and went straight to an agency, as if she were staffing a war zone. It didn't matter. Every single one of them quit. I made it my personal mission to break them. I wasn't trying to get attention. I wasn't acting out for love. I was testing how long someone would stay once they realized I was relentless. When they showered, I flushed the toilet on purpose, over and over, just to mess with the water temperature. Sometimes I'd wait until I heard them yelp and then do it again. Other times, I'd throw whatever I could find over the curtain. Toys. Wet towels. Once, an entire roll of toilet paper I'd unraveled down the hallway first, just to make it dramatic. I learned their routines fast. What time did they relax? At what time do they let their guard down? I'd hide behind doors and jump out screaming, not once, but repeatedly, until their nerves were fried. I'd stand silently in doorways at night, just staring, long enough for them to notice me and panic. If they locked the door, I'd knock. If they ignored it, I'd knock harder. If they told me to stop, I'd stop just long enough to make them think it was over. Then I'd start again. I'd move their things. Just enough that they'd question themselves. Shoes are in the wrong place. Keys not where they swore they left them. I'd swear I didn't touch anything and look them dead in the eye while doing it. Calm. Convincing. Like I believed my own lie. Some of them cried. One yelled at Micky. One packed her bags in the middle of the day and left without saying goodbye. Another made it to the end of the week, sat down at the kitchen table, and told my mom she couldn't do it anymore. That there was something wrong with me. She wasn't wrong. But no one ever asked why I was like that. They just kept replacing them. New face. Same outcome. I didn't need to be loud. I didn't need to be violent. I just needed to make them leave. And I always won. Then one day, she brought a man home. His name was Kevin. There was no explanation. No introduction. One day, he was just there. Sleeping on the couch. Becoming part of the house by default. I was eight years old, and I did not know what to think of him. He was kind. Quiet. He slept a lot. His hands shook sometimes. He seemed nervous, like his body never fully relaxed. I later learned that Kevin had been one of Micky's patients at the mental hospital. She was his nurse. He had been discharged, and she brought him home. Kevin was a recovering heroin addict. At the time, I did not understand what that meant. I just knew that my mother drove him to a clinic every day. I sat in the backseat of her old 1990s Honda Accord while he went inside to get his medication. When I asked what it was for, he smiled and told me it helped clear the cobwebs. Kevin told me stories sometimes. About his past. About drugs. About voices in his head. About trying to jump out of a window at the hospital and how Micky stopped him. Whatever happened between them, they fell in love. To me, he was simply a man who stayed. I did not understand it then, but that was the beginning of me having a father. Not the one I was born to, but the first one who showed up. The first one who occupied space in my life long enough to matter.

And that was the moment the trajectory of my life began to shift. As my life with Kevin began, I remember one day that confused me more than it scared me. I was eight years old. We were driving somewhere unfamiliar. Far from the Hollywood Hills. Far from tennis courts and quiet streets. Kevin took us down a long road lined with tents. It was Skid Row, though I did not know the name then. I only knew it felt like another world. Everything looked dirty. The ground. The buildings. The people. They moved differently. Slower. Heavier. Like they were carrying something I could not see. I had never seen people like that before. Kevin stopped the car and picked up a woman named Molly. He said she was his best friend. She looked rough. Tired. Older than her age. She did not talk much. He brought her home with us, and she slept in our living room for days. She barely moved. I remember stepping around her as if she were furniture that had suddenly appeared. When she finally woke up, Kevin stayed close to her. Talking softly. Encouraging her. Trying to get her to come to church with us. I did not understand what was happening. I only knew something serious was unfolding, something adults did not explain to children.

After that, I started to notice things.

Not all at once. Slowly. The way kids do, when they don't yet have the language for what they're seeing. Kevin was trying to be good. I could feel that. He woke up early. He went to meetings. He prayed. He talked about God as if God were someone who had pulled him back from the edge and was still holding his sleeve. He wanted to help people the way he had been helped. Sometimes that meant bringing the mess home with him. Our house became a place where broken people passed through. Not all the time, but enough for me to understand that something about us made people think they could rest there for a moment. I saw exhaustion up close. Desperation. Gratitude mixed with shame. I saw adults cry in ways I had never seen before, quiet and embarrassed, like they were apologizing just for existing. I did not understand addiction, but I understood need. I understood that some people wanted relief more than rules. More than safety. More than tomorrow. Kevin tried to explain things to me in simple terms. He told me some people were sick in ways you could not see. That some people needed help even when they pushed it away. He never spoke badly about them. Not once. Even when they disappeared. Even when they chose the street over a bed. That stayed with me. At the same time, Micky's rules did not soften. Church was still mandatory. Obedience was still enforced. God was still watching. There was no room for questions. No room for confusion. And yet, suddenly, there were people in our lives who did not fit into any of the categories I had been taught. They were not righteous. They were not evil. They were just hurting. That contradiction sat heavily in my chest. I started to feel as if I were living between worlds. One foot in strict order. One foot in chaos. On one side, rules and punishment. On the other, suffering and mercy. And in the middle, a quiet man

who was trying to stay clean and help others do the same. Kevin did not raise his voice. He did not hit. He did not demand obedience. He asked questions. He listened. When he made mistakes, he admitted them. That alone felt radical to me.

I began to watch him closely. Not because I wanted to be him exactly, but because I was trying to understand what a man was supposed to be. The men I had seen before were distant, untouchable, or mythical. Kevin was real. Flawed. Present. Trying. I noticed how people responded to him. How they trusted him. How they leaned into his calm. I noticed how my body felt around him. Less tense. Less alert. Like I could breathe a little deeper when he was in the room. That was new. I did not think of it as safety at the time. I just knew it felt different. Looking back, I realize that was the moment my nervous system started learning something else. That chaos was not the only language. That strength did not always announce itself loudly. That masculinity did not have to look like control, fear, or dominance. I was still eight years old. I still did not understand most of what was happening. But I was absorbing it all. Every contradiction. Every quiet lesson. Every example of who I could become. And without realizing it, I was already choosing. As Kevin settled into our lives and quietly became my father, everything started to loosen. Not all at once. But enough to feel it. The rules in our house began to soften. The strange ones. The ones that never made sense. I stopped eating on the floor off paper bags. I was suddenly allowed to sit at the table like a normal kid. Kevin cooked real meals. Food that smelled good. Food that didn't feel like punishment. Suddenly, I was allowed outside. That was new.

I could play in the neighborhood until dark. We lived in North Hollywood then, and for the first time, the world felt reachable. I would run door to door, asking other kids to come out and play. That was my first real experience making friends. No supervision. No fear of doing something wrong just by existing. Just bikes, sidewalks, scraped knees, and fun until the sun went down. Kevin made life with Micky more bearable. She worked constantly. Double shifts. Extra hours. Always tired. Always gone. Nursing consumed her. Her dream was simple and relentless. Get us out of California. Somewhere quieter.

Somewhere cheaper. Somewhere, she believed God wanted us to be. That was where everything was headed. Leaving California. Kevin had issues. A lot of them. But he was a good man. He had long, thick brown hair. The kind people noticed. He was skinny. About five-ten.

Traditionally good-looking. The kind of guy who could get women easily, and often did, even when he wasn't trying. But unlike Jameson, Kevin didn't wear power comfortably. Jameson had money. Fame. Control. Women moved around him like proof of success. Kevin was different.

He had the looks, but not the armor. He was charming, but fragile. A man shaped by damage instead of privilege. His childhood lived inside him in ways he couldn't shut off. It made him gentle. It also made him breakable. If Jameson taught me how men dominate the world, Kevin taught me how men survive it. Both lessons stayed with me. And I didn't know it yet, but I was already learning how to move between those two versions of myself. Kevin wasn't the loudest man in the room. He wasn't the safest bet. He wasn't the kind of choice people expected from a woman like Micky. But Micky didn't choose men the way other women did. She wasn't drawn to ease or certainty. She was drawn to gravity. To intensity. To something that felt like fate instead of comfort. She carried herself like someone who had already lived through too much and wasn't interested in pretending otherwise. There was warmth in her, but it came with edges. Laughter that could disarm you. Silence that could shut a room down. She was magnetic without trying, powerful without announcing it. People wanted her. Constantly. But she never acted like she owed anyone anything. She loved Kevin fiercely, stubbornly, and without apology. Even when it cost her. Even when it didn't make sense. Even when it set the trajectory for everything that came after.

Looking back, I think that was the first lesson I ever learned about love. That wanting isn't the same as choosing, and that sometimes is the most beautiful.

Sometimes people pick the hardest paths on purpose. Kevin and Micky slept in separate rooms. He slept on the couch sometimes. Other nights in the spare room. I noticed it right away. I remember him taking showers, and Micky never going in there with him.

They moved around each other carefully, like there were rules I didn't understand yet. I asked about it once. Why don't you guys sleep together in the same bed? Kevin smiled, almost embarrassed, and told me they weren't allowed to be together like that until they were married. That was his faith. His discipline. His way of trying to do things right for Micky. After a few months of Kevin being around and life slowly feeling more normal, the big day finally came. I was eight years old. I was dressed in a little tuxedo. We went up to Beverly Hills with Jameson for the wedding. It was massive. Overwhelming. There were celebrities everywhere. People I had seen on television. Actors. Familiar faces. Kids I recognized from auditions, from pilots I had been in myself. I had done a few TV projects as a child. Nothing that went anywhere, but enough to recognize the world. It confused me. How could people be on TV and also standing right in front of me?

The room felt unreal. Like a set. Like something staged just for us. When Kevin and Micky stood at the altar, everything else faded. They stared at each other as if nothing else existed. It didn't look like real-life love. It looked like movie love. The kind you assume is exaggerated until you see it up close. I was the ring bearer. I walked down the aisle holding the rings, surrounded by hundreds of people watching me. I remember feeling small and important at the same time. Like I had wandered into something much bigger than myself. Like this moment mattered more than I understood. They got married. And just like that, Kevin became my father. Not biologically. Not perfectly. But officially.

He gave me something I had never had before. A man who chose me. A name to stand under. A place to land. I didn't know what that would cost later. I only knew that for the first time in my life, I belonged to something that felt real.

2

RICHES TO RAGS

All of a sudden, I had a father.

Kevin was good to us. Consistently. He did the things fathers are supposed to do, the things that quietly add up. He took me to North Hollywood Park daily. He walked me to the 7-Eleven almost every day for candy and comic books. It wasn't extravagant. It was routine. And that was the point. Routine meant stability. Stability was new. Kevin's world felt foreign to me. I came from tennis courts and mansions, from quiet wealth and unspoken rules. His world was made up of halfway houses, meetings, and people counting days. People trying to stay clean one day at a time. I didn't understand it yet, but I could feel the shift. It was a different gravity. When I was 10, he introduced me to his best friend, Mitchell. Mitchell lived in a halfway house. I didn't know what that really meant, only that it wasn't temporary and it wasn't freedom. It was a place for people who had already fallen and were trying not to fall again.

Mitchell was calm. Observant. He spoke carefully, like words mattered. He treated me like a person, not a problem. At the time, he was just another man in Kevin's orbit, another figure passing through this unfamiliar world. I had no idea how important he would become. Not then. Later. In ways that would shape the rest of my life. As I began to spend time with my new father. One day, we were at the park. I started climbing to the top of the jungle gym like I did every day. Far away, I noticed a little girl watching me. I caught myself staring at her back. I didn't know what it was yet, but I know now that it was probably the first crush I ever had. The first time I noticed the opposite sex noticing me, and I noticed back, she was just standing there, looking up at me in awe. My eleven-year-old brain made a simple decision. I'll climb to the top. I'll jump. I'll impress her. I slowly reached the top, made eye contact, and then jumped. I felt like a rockstar doing it. I didn't know it then, but it had rained the night before. The sand was packed hard, almost like concrete. I hit the ground, hard, and felt pain I didn't know was possible. It wasn't sharp at first. It was a total collapse. Every bone in my right foot snapped. The pain was so intense I thought once again I was dying. Kevin ran to me, screaming in panic. He dropped to the ground beside me, panicked, shaking, trying to keep me still. I saw a look in his eyes I had never seen before. He was scared. He was there. Kevin was always there. Four plates. Sixteen screws. Two surgeries. Six months without walking. Teaching me to walk again. Kevin never left. That was the first time I learned something important, even if I didn't understand it yet. Risk felt natural to me. Pain felt survivable, and when everything went wrong, Kevin was there to pick me up. I didn't know it then, but those patterns would follow me for a long time. Micky was still always at the hospital. For a couple of years, she worked nonstop, saving to buy a house. Kevin held things together at home. We lived in an apartment with a family upstairs. The mother's name was Faith; she acted as if she despised us. Dirty looks every time she saw us, especially Micky. This went on for a year. Kevin had a motorhome he loved. He was always working on it, cleaning it, talking about it. It was his escape. Somewhere that felt like his. Then the notes started. They were left on the motorhome. Love notes. Telling him how amazing he was. How much someone admired him. How in love they were with him. The handwriting never changed. Neither did the message. They went on for months. Kevin never responded. Not once. He never entertained it. The notes didn't stop. Eventually, Kevin decided to end it. He left a note of his own. Told them to meet him at the nearby park, inside the motorhome, at a specific time. On the day of the meeting, Kevin parked the motorhome and walked away. Inside, waiting, was Micky. The door slowly opened as Micky sat at the table just waiting. Like an animal slowly waiting for her chance to attack. Breath slow but ramping up as she waited for the door to open. The door opened. In walked Faith. She was dressed in her best. A white dress. Full makeup. Like she was going out for the night. Like she thought this would change her life. When Faith saw Micky sitting there, her face went white. Like she'd seen a ghost. Micky sat there like she wanted her to feel every second of this before she moved. She stood up slowly and with purpose, then violently shoved Faith out of the motorhome. Faith flew out and hit the ground hard. Faith was gasping for air and vomited all over herself. She felt as pathetic and small as she looked. Micky threw the letters all over her as she lay on the ground. White dress covered in blood and vomit. Micky spat in her face and growled like a snarling animal, "Stay the fuck away from my husband, bitch." I was eleven years old. This is where I learned about loyalty, pain, and revenge. Sometimes I would see my grandmother, Jennifer. She was estranged from most of the family. Distance followed her everywhere, even when she was physically present. She spent most of her life in the limelight. Rich. Fast. Almost famous, but never quite there. Always close enough to touch it, never close enough to keep it. She lived in Elizabeth Taylor's shadow. Being her double in most of her movies. She traveled in the same circles. Same proximity. That kind of almost-success does something to a person. Jennifer was an alcoholic. Deeply. Functionally. The kind that hides in plain sight because money and charm cover the damage. She was hard on my mother, Micky. I understand now why Micky was hard on me, her firstborn. Jennifer carried a dark energy. Even as a kid, I could feel it. Some adults feel unsafe without ever raising their voice. When I stayed the night at her house, she made me sleep in the bathroom. I had a Transformers blanket and a matching pair of pajamas. She made me lie on the floor near the tub. In the living room, on her dining room table, I noticed bottles everywhere. Alcohol on the table and a large bowl sitting out in the open.

I asked her once what the bowl was for.

She told me it was for "all the keys, silly."

One night, I couldn't sleep. I snuck out of the bathroom and watched from upstairs. Countless couples came in and out. They were laughing. Drinking. Loud. Dressed like they were important in designer clothing. When they arrived, they dropped their keys into the bowl. They danced, drank, and did lines of cocaine. I saw women playing the board game Twister, but getting naked with men while doing it. I saw a couple having sex in the middle of the room, and everyone was standing around watching like it was a show. When they were ready to leave, someone would reach in, grab a random set, and go home with whoever owned them. I was eleven years old. I didn't know the word for it then. I know it now. A key party. Jennifer lived that lifestyle. Fame-adjacent. Alcohol-soaked. Detached. Dark. The old Hollywood lifestyle, ritual things done in secret that everyone knew but never talked about. She shaped Micky, and through her, she shaped me. As I grew, I had a lot of experiences with bullies in my life, and the first one I can clearly remember happened when I was eleven years old. I went to a very large church in Los Angeles. The kind filled with famous people and actors. Adults who smiled too much. Kids who already knew where they ranked. There was a boy my age there. His father was a very famous stuntman known for films like Indiana Jones and Lethal Weapon. Martial arts. Stunts. Toughness. His son carried that energy like a weapon. That boy terrorized me. Every Sunday, he made sure I knew I didn't belong. I was innocent. I loved God. When people danced, I danced. I felt it and that made me an easy target.

He mocked me. Called me a Mexican jumping bean. His friends laughed. He had a little gang around him. For months, they chipped away at me. Made fun of my hair. My body. Called me fat. Called me weird. That boy is famous now. He's an actor. He's all over Netflix. I won't say his name. What matters is this: he shaped my first experience with self-doubt. With insecurity. With learning that confidence can be taken from you. That was the first time I remember feeling bad about myself. The bullying didn't stop there. It went on for months. Quietly at first, then openly. Every Sunday. Every event. Anywhere he could find me. He'd find a way to point me out. If I were smiling, he'd turn it into something to mock. I was still kind back then. Still innocent. Still open. I hadn't learned how to protect myself yet.

And in that world, people could sense it.

Looking back, I see it clearly now. That wasn't just bullying. That was the first time I encountered predators. People who feed off insecurity. People who need to diminish others to feel powerful. That boy was just the beginning. I never forgot him. I still see his face everywhere now. On Netflix. In movies. Successful. Celebrated. Elevated.

It's strange how easily people can treat others like nothing and still rise to the top.

But that's exactly why my mother didn't want that life for me. She wanted to save my innocence before it was stripped away completely. It's 1997, LA. Walking down the street, you saw huge billboards of "Titanic." Micky and Kevin have their first son, Karl. She kept working her fingers to the bone. Her one goal was to get me, Karl and Kevin out of California. Out of the life. Out of the darkness. She always told me stories about old Hollywood parties she'd been to. Dark things. Things no one talks about. She said some of her girlfriends disappeared and were never heard from again. She talked about secret sex parties. About corruption hiding behind glamour. She would talk about old rituals, sacrifice, about how children were sacrificed to false gods for fame and beauty. About how Hollywood rots you from the inside if you stay close to it long enough. She didn't want that life for Karl or me. She didn't want the darkness she grew up around to touch us. So she worked and worked and worked. Countless hours. Long shifts. Missed sleep. All to save fifty thousand dollars for a down payment. She refused Jameson's help. She was proud. If she didn't earn it herself, it didn't count. Eventually, she got the money together. In her mind, she was saving her family. Leaving California. Leaving Hollywood. Leaving the shadows she knew too well. She wanted land. Space. Quiet. A simple life. Then one day, everything we owned was packed into the motorhome. And the drive to Oregon began. This was only the beginning.

3

THE FARM

WE MOVED TO OREGON when I was fourteen. Right before we left, my biological father tried to get custody of me. I remember the courtroom more than anything else. The way it smelled was old and sterile. The way Micky sat stiff beside me, already angry. I remember seeing him for the first time in years. John. Smaller than I expected. Quieter. He didn't look like the man I had been warned about my whole childhood. He didn't look like a monster. That's what Micky always said. He beat her when she was pregnant. That he was dangerous. A Yugoslavian man with a violent past. Gangs. Fights. A hit was put on his head. He was blinded in one eye. Forced to leave Yugoslavia because gangs had a price on his head. That was the story. That was the version I grew up with. I never questioned it because I wasn't allowed to. I wasn't allowed to talk to him. I wasn't allowed to ask. The story was already decided. Seeing him in that courtroom didn't clarify anything. It made everything worse. I don't remember what the judge said. I don't remember the ruling. I don't remember who won or lost. What I remember is that we left almost immediately after, like we were running from something. California disappeared behind us. Oregon felt like another planet. Everything was green, too green. The weather didn't make sense. Cold and warm on the same day. Rain without warning, then sun immediately after. It was quiet. Too quiet. The kind of quiet that makes you feel exposed. What hit me first wasn't the cold. It was the people. Everyone was white. I had never seen anything like it. No familiar faces. No familiar energy. It felt less like moving and more like being dropped somewhere I didn't belong. Like I had crossed into a place where I wasn't supposed to ask questions about who I was or where I came from. I didn't know if my mother had protected me from John or taken something from me. I just knew that something important had been decided without me and that was the beginning of understanding that adults don't always tell the truth. But they are very good at making it sound final. We didn't just move. We disappeared. They took us into the middle of nowhere. A town called Selma. One of those places that barely registers on a map. The kind of town you don't end up in unless you're trying to get away or run from something. There was almost nothing there. A grocery store that closed early. A post office. A small market that sold the same dusty snacks year-round. One gas station. That was it. The nearest real city, Grants Pass, was half an hour away. There was nowhere to go and nothing to do. Just distance.

Our house was big. Too big. Around four thousand square feet, sitting on five acres, as if it were trying to justify its own existence. It was nice. New. Quiet.

Everything Micky ever wanted. Everything Kevin always talked about. Land. Space. Privacy. They finally got it. It felt like a trade had been made without asking me. Like adults had decided their lives were starting over and mine was just collateral. I didn't understand what was happening yet. I didn't know how school worked. I didn't know how anything worked. I just knew I had been dropped somewhere unfamiliar and told this was home now. No warning. No transition. No explanation made it make sense.

One day, there was noise, movement, and familiarity. The next day, there was land and silence and a house that echoed. It didn't feel like a fresh start. It felt like something had detonated, and we were standing in the smoke, waiting for someone to explain what was gone. No one did. Once we were settled, Micky stopped working. Not slowly. Not reluctantly. She just decided she was done. The state became her cash cow. State programs. Checks. Welfare. Food stamps, whatever could be pulled without being questioned too closely. She was tired. Burned out. She had already paid her dues, at least in her mind. This was her turn to take a break. Kevin never had a career to abandon. He bought an old Chevy LUV pickup from the eighties and drove it everywhere. He was good with people. Everyone liked him. He smiled easily. Talked easily. He fixed things. Cars. Fences. Whatever needed hands. He would also make handmade canes out of driftwood for extra money. He moved through town doing odd jobs, never staying anywhere long enough for it to feel permanent. That was the structure. If you could call it that. We went from excess to the absence of it immediately. I had lived around money before. Real money. Mansions. Tennis courts. People whose names carried weight. Then, suddenly, I was layering shirts with holes in them to stay warm. Shoes were splitting at the seams. Nothing dramatic happened. It just thinned out. Comfort first. Then dignity. Then expectation. I learned early how fast a life can invert. How quickly abundance becomes something you're not supposed to talk about anymore. Like it never really happened. Barely fourteen. I didn't have language for any of it yet. I just knew when something didn't feel right, even if I couldn't explain why. A few doors down, there was a farm called "Healthy Farms." Walking down the driveway to a new, enormous house, there was a big sign in the front like it was important. I walked down the driveway and met two elderly men who lived there. They were in their 70s, named Clarence and Elwood. After a quick interview, Clarence immediately hired me for one dollar an hour. It was 1999. I worked there every day, just trying to make money for clothes so that I at least looked like I belonged. At first, it was fine. Then, as time went on, I started noticing Clarence watching me. Not casually. Not in passing. I would be outside working, weed-whacking, feeding animals, doing whatever needed to be done. I would feel it first almost immediately. The pressure between my shoulders, the hairs on the back of my neck raised. Then I'd look up and see him standing at the window. Still. Silent. It felt like something was about to happen, but I didn't know what. Just watching, always watching. Sometimes he gave me extra money. No reason. No explanation. He'd press it into my hand and smile like it was normal. Like it meant something I was supposed to understand. It made my stomach tighten. It felt like too much. Like something was being exchanged that I hadn't agreed to. He was overly nice. Too attentive. He kept finding reasons to be close. To linger. To talk longer than necessary. He rubbed my shoulders and put his fingers through my hair. Once he told me I could work without my shirt on, he said, "That's how real men do it." I said no. He laughed it off like it was nothing, then brought it up again later, like I needed to, like it was required. That was when I started paying attention. Elwood and Clarence acted like there was something sealed off about them. Something private. Like they lived by a different set of rules once you were on their property. It wasn't aggressive. It was calm. Polite. Which somehow made it worse. One day, I walked into a room and saw Elwood and Clarence together in a way I didn't understand. I had never seen adult men do that before, and I froze. I didn't know what I was looking at. I didn't know what it meant. No one had ever explained anything like that to me. Clarence sat me down afterward. He spoke slowly. Carefully. As if he were teaching me something important. He told me he was different. He told me it was normal. Then he told me something that confused me so deeply I didn't know where to put it.

He said he had male and female genitalia. He said that's why everything made sense for what I saw. He said that's why nothing about it was wrong. He said it like it was biology, like it was fact. Like it was a fact I just hadn't learned yet. I remember nodding, because that's what kids do when adults speak with confidence. Inside, I was panicking. I didn't know what was real. I didn't know what was being explained and what was being invented. I didn't know why my body felt like it needed to leave, even though nothing violent had happened. After that, the watching got worse. Windows. Doorways. Long pauses where I could feel eyes on me, even when I couldn't see anyone. I started choosing where I stood. How long did I stay? When I

left. I didn't know why yet. I just knew my body was paying attention even if my mind wasn't. At the time, I didn't know what grooming was. I didn't know that adults could slowly rewrite reality and call it education. I only knew I was a kid, surrounded by people crossing lines without ever naming them. That place didn't feel dangerous because it was chaotic. It felt dangerous because it was calm. Organized. Certain. Like everything had already been decided, and I was the last one to find out. Whatever was happening there didn't announce itself. It didn't rush. It didn't need to. It watched. It waited. It let me stay.

And by the time I understood that something was wrong, I was already inside it. One day, Kevin picked me up for work and walked me over to the house. Clarence was there. Elwood too. It felt casual. Normal. Just men talking in a driveway. Nothing about it looked dangerous. But after that day, everything shifted. Not all at once. Slowly. Quietly. The kind of change you don't notice until you can't remember how things used to be. Kevin started spending his days there. At first, just helping out. Fixing things. Talking. Then every day. All day. He was finally making real money. More than he

ever had before. It gave him something he hadn't had in a long time. Purpose.

Direction. Somewhere to be. He wasn't the same. It wasn't dramatic. He didn't become mean or loud. He just felt different. Distracted. Less present. Like part of him stayed behind when he came home. Sometimes I worked there with him. Sometimes I didn't. But when I did, I noticed things I hadn't before.

Kevin worked with his shirt off. No big deal. It was hot. Then I thought maybe I should, too. Like it was just how things were done there. That's when I saw

Clarence again.

Standing at the window.

Not moving. Not reacting. Just watching. Touching himself in ways I didn't understand, the same look. Dead eyes, sinister even. Empty. Focused. Like he wasn't seeing us as people anymore. Like he was looking through us. It got worse as time went on. Kevin started drinking with them at night. Staying late. Coming home later and later. Sometimes not coming home at all. Micky noticed before I did. She always did. The house changed when he stopped being around. The fights started small. Then they didn't stop. I'd come home and hear them screaming. Doors slamming. Voices sharp enough to cut through walls. One night, I heard Micky say it. Clear as anything.

"He's in love with you." The words didn't make sense. Kevin had adopted me by then. He was officially my father. My real one, at least on paper. I didn't even know how to hold the idea in my head. How could Clarence be in love with my dad? How could my dad be in love with anyone but Micky? I remember Micky yelling, telling him if he wanted to be over there all the time, then he should just go be with him. I remember Kevin not denying it. Just standing there. Silent. I didn't understand what I was hearing. I didn't understand what any of it meant. I just knew something adult and dangerous was happening right in front of me, and no one was explaining it.

After a while, Kevin stopped coming home. He started living at Clarence's house. No one ever told me why. No one explained what was happening over there. I just knew he wasn't with us anymore. And the longer he stayed gone, the heavier everything felt.

There was something about that place that didn't quite feel right. Like once you crossed onto that property, things changed in ways you couldn't undo. Micky was furious. Scared. Unraveling. Eventually, she made me stop working there. At the time, it felt sudden. Cruel. Like another thing taken away without warning. Only later did I understand. She wasn't punishing me. She was pulling me out. Whatever was happening at that house wasn't just breaking their marriage. It was swallowing people whole. I didn't know what Kevin was involved in. I didn't know what promises were being made. I didn't know which lines had been crossed once the doors closed and the lights went out. I only knew that the man who had just become my father was gone. And the place that took him didn't give things back. Six months later one night, a quiet night, it was raining. Not hard. Just enough to soak everything slowly. I hadn't seen Kevin much by then. Months, maybe. He had been gone more than he'd been home. Six months of absence, unexplained. He existed somewhere else now. Somewhere we didn't talk about.

Then I heard a truck. Headlights cutting down the driveway. Slow. Careful. Like he wasn't sure he was supposed to be there. Micky went outside before I did. I stayed back, watching from the dark.

Kevin was sitting in the driver's seat with the engine running. He hadn't gotten out. He was hunched forward, his forehead pressed against the steering wheel, shaking. Crying in a way I had never seen before. Not quietly. Not controlled. Like something had finally broken loose. Rain streaked down the windshield. His face was twisted. Raw. I saw his mouth move.

"I'm sorry. I'll never go back there. I can't live without you." He started promising to never leave. Micky started crying too. Kevin opened the door and stepped out into the rain. He walked toward her like he was exhausted just from standing. He put his hands on her face gently, like she might disappear if he didn't hold her there. He looked at her for a long time. Too long. Then she grabbed him. They held each other in the driveway, rain soaking through their clothes, crying and kissing like it was a scene from a movie that didn't explain itself. Like whatever had happened offscreen was too dangerous to show, to even talk about. And just like that, he was back. No explanation. No conversation. No questions answered. Kevin came home that night and never spoke about where he had been or what had happened to him. Whatever he left behind stayed unnamed. But he didn't come back the same. Something had followed him home. You could feel it in the way he moved. The way he went quiet. The house never fully settled again.

I was too young to understand what he had escaped. I only knew that whatever had happened over there had hollowed him out. And whatever it was, it never let him go completely.

4

LUCIFER, NAMED JACK

AFTER KEVIN CAME BACK down the driveway, things did not fall apart. They held. Around that time, Mitchell moved up from LA to Oregon and lived with us for about a year or two. It was the end of the nineties, and the world was holding its breath. Y2K was coming. If you weren't alive then, it's hard to explain how real the fear felt. Computers everywhere had been programmed with two-digit years. Ninety-nine instead of nineteen ninety-nine. When the calendar rolled over to two thousand, people believed all systems would fail. Banks. Power grids. Planes. Hospitals. Military systems. No one knew what would break or how bad it would get. The fear wasn't just that things would glitch. It was as if everything would stop at once. No electricity. No money. No food. No order.

The news talked about it constantly. Experts argued on TV. Some said it would be nothing. Others said it would be the end of modern life. And the people who believed the worst believed it completely. Mitchell was one of them. He ran a Y2K survival supply company. An online business, before that, was even an uncommon thing. The guest bedroom became his office. The garage became a bunker. Floor-to-ceiling survival gear. Water purification systems. Gas masks. Medical kits. Flashlights. Generators. Ammo. Guns, food buckets stacked like bricks, enough for twenty years of survival. Enough to survive a collapse. Enough to outlast chaos. We weren't preparing for inconvenience.

We were preparing for the end. Living in that house, surrounded by it, the fear soaked into everything. Conversations were about timelines. About what would fail first. About how fast things would turn violent once the lights went out. Even as a kid, I absorbed it. I felt it in my chest. The sense that something huge was coming and no one could stop it. New Year's Eve arrived. We gathered around the TV like it was a countdown to judgment. Ten. Nine.

Eight. I remember my heart pounding. Not excitement. Fear. Real fear. I truly believed the world might end when the clock struck midnight. That the power would cut. That the house would go dark. That sirens would start. That everything we knew would disappear in a single second. Five. Four. Three. Two. One. Happy New Year. Nothing happened. The lights stayed on.

The TV kept playing. The house didn't shake. The world didn't end. I remember the confusion more than the relief. The way my body didn't know how to stand down. Like it had been bracing for impact and never got permission to relax. The fear didn't disappear instantly. It just had nowhere to go. I never forgot that moment.

Standing there, surrounded by survival gear, realizing the apocalypse we had prepared for didn't come. How real the fear had felt. How convincing it had been. How deeply it had embedded itself in us. It was the first time I learned something that would repeat throughout my life. You can prepare endlessly for disaster. You can live inside fear and the thing you're bracing for still might never arrive. But the fear stays with you anyway. By the year 2000, Karl was three. He moved through the house like it was permanent. Like it belonged to him. He knew which doors stuck. Which floorboards creaked. Which adults meant what they said and which ones didn't. He assumed the house would always be there.

That same year, Micky and Kevin had another son, Kasey, who arrived quietly. Newborn. Small. Always being held. He changed the way people stood in rooms. Even Kevin slowed down around him. Not out of tenderness. Out of awareness. It mattered that this was Micky's second set of kids. I came from the first version of her life. Before Kevin. Before anything softened. I grew up inside rules that shifted without warning. Discipline that arrived already angry. Religion that pressed itself into everything. Fear passed off as structure. By the time things calmed down, whatever was going to stick had already. Karl and Kasey did not grow up in a house of weird rules and religious scorn. They grew up with Kevin. With routine. With predictability. With a man who stayed where he was supposed to stay. There were no beatings. No sermons that bled into punishment. No sense that love could be withdrawn without explanation. What they had passed for normal. Karl never learned how to brace a hit; Kasey never had to. I carried what came before. I felt it constantly. I carried it quietly. There were three of us kids in the house, but we were not raised the same. For a while, the family looked intact. Holidays returned. Christmas happened. Lights went up. Decorations came out. Boxes opened and closed. The house filled with people, noise and movement. It looked like life. Games were played. Arguments were constant and never stopped. Laughter happened without effort. Plates stacked in the sink. Music drifted between rooms. Nothing broke or felt broken. That passed for stability. Karl trusted the adults around him without knowing it was a risk. When he fell, someone caught him. Kasey was the baby everyone protected. From the outside, Kevin and Micky looked like the family they had always wanted. Kevin stayed.

Micky stopped her abrasive ways. The edges dulled. They did not fully disappear. They waited. No one spoke about what came before. Not the leaving. Not the yelling. Not the driveway. The past stayed where it was because everyone agreed not to touch it.

That year does not announce itself in memory. It does not ask to be understood. It simply exists. Quiet. Functional. Convincing enough to believe. Which is why it mattered.

I was fourteen. Homeschooled my whole life. I got a scholarship to a private Christian school in Grants Pass. For the first time, I was going to real school. I was excited. Not because I knew what I was doing, but because I wanted something I had never had: friends. A life outside the house. A life outside Micky. A woman who ran Bible studies, who measured everything in verses and discipline. I wanted people who weren't just her. We were poor. I had no clothes. I remember going to Goodwill, picking through whatever was left. They gave me old jeans and a polo dress shirt, three sizes too big. I was short. Five-two. Chubby. Acne on my face. Hair grown out, parted down the middle. I looked like someone who didn't quite know himself, and it showed. I didn't know how to talk to anyone. I had never learned. My whole life had been structured around study and rules. I didn't have social skills. I didn't have confidence. I didn't have a life outside my mother's shadow. And yet, I was stepping into it. Stepping into a world I had never touched, a place I wanted to belong. The first week was a fight I didn't know how to fight. I couldn't make friends. I couldn't talk to girls. Every attempt to speak landed flat, or worse, they laughed or ignored me. I tripped over words I didn't know how to use. I didn't understand the rhythm of their jokes, their whispers, their glances. Everyone else already had language I hadn't been taught. I was a social pariah, invisible in plain sight, wandering the hallways like I didn't belong, and in every stare, every passing hand, every empty seat, it hit me harder. I was on the outside, and no one was letting me in. As I tried to navigate school, there was this boy in my grade named Jack. We were all still kids, barely teenagers, but Jack was something else. Six feet tall, built like he spent every hour in a gym daily, a face sharp enough to belong on a poster. He had that effortless surfer look, the kind of good looks that made every girl swoon and every boy want to be him. He was the best at sports, grades, jokes, the whole package. And me? I was invisible. Small. Soft. Clumsy. I didn't know it yet, but Jack was going to carve every one of my insecurities into me like graffiti on stone, and some of those marks are still there today. Jack did not bully me just once. He made it his mission. Every day, every hallway, every classroom, every corner of the school, he found me. He shoved my head into lockers, knocked books from my hands, and slapped my head from behind when I wasn't looking. He humiliated me in front of everyone, and he did it with a smile. I didn't know it then, but I recognize it now. He was a classic narcissist. He needed someone smaller than him. Someone weaker. Someone to feed on. He fed off my pain. Every flinch, every tear, every moment I froze under his gaze, it fueled him. It got him high. He loved it. On the bus, he made sure I couldn't escape. He turned rides into performances. He shouted my name, my weight, my face, anything he could find, until the entire bus was cheering the same slurs with him on repeat. I was the spectacle. The entertainment. Every chant, every call-out, every mocking laugh drilled into me that I was alone. That everyone hated me, or at least that Jack had convinced them to, and Jack thrived. Every reaction of mine was a hit. Every second I suffered, he inhaled it like air, smiling wider with each humiliation.

I cried after school every day. Alone in my room. Lying in bed, staring at the ceiling, thinking maybe it would be easier not to exist anymore. That was the first time those thoughts ever came to me, not the last. I didn't have the language for it yet. I just wanted the pain to stop. I was innocent. I had never experienced cruelty like this. I didn't know someone could enjoy dismantling another person so completely. The only thing that kept me anchored was my family. I told myself I still had Micky. I still had Kevin. I still had Karl and Kasey. I told myself love at home could outweigh hatred everywhere else. I was still naïve enough to believe that.

One day, I walked up to my locker, and there was a letter stuck in the side halfway. It was from a girl named Blaire. She was the prettiest girl in the school; everyone wanted her. Every time she walked into a room, it was like a dream. She walked like she floated, as if she belonged in a dream. She lived in my dreams every night. Note after note, again and again, always from her. Folded neatly and slipped into my locker. Careful handwriting. Sweet words. She told me she liked me. That she wanted to kiss me, to love me. That if I did certain things, she would reward me. Put a flower under the vending machine. Buy her a Britney Spears CD and leave it in her desk. Do this, and I'll be with you. Do that, and I'll give you everything you have ever dreamed of. Do this, and I'll go with you to the dance. I did everything she asked daily. Over and over again for months. Finally, she asked me to meet her in secluded spots in the school several times. Every time I showed up. And every time, she didn't. I told myself she was shy. Nervous. Busy. I didn't understand yet that I was being played, set up, and played with by a predator as evil as Satan himself. Someone watching, orchestrating the entire thing behind the scenes like a puppet master. The day she finally showed up, I saw Jack standing behind her, holding her like she was his, with the devilish grin on his face. I knew immediately the whole thing was a setup. He grabbed her hard by the hair and kissed her even harder. Right in front of me, my heart dropped. Then, out of nowhere, the rest of my class appeared. Cameras already raised. Fingers pointing. Laughter breaking open all at once. Everything hit me in waves. The notes. The tasks. The waiting. It had all been Jack. The entire thing. Planned. Orchestrated. A setup. I turned red instantly. My face burned. I started crying before I could stop myself. Someone threw water onto the front of my pants and took a picture. Another voice shouted that I had peed myself. They laughed harder. They took more pictures from the side, from the front, documenting every second of it. I stood there shaking, humiliated beyond words, knowing this moment would follow me long after the bell rang. That was almost the worst part. Not the laughter. Not the cameras. But the realization that Jack didn't just want to hurt me in passing.

He wanted to study me. Manipulate me. Break me slowly. Publicly. Thoroughly. Showing my face in that school after that was a daily battle. Every day after that felt like war. I woke up bracing for what he would do next. Jack shaped the battlefield and decided the rules. He didn't just hurt me. He taught me how easily the world could be turned against you, how cruelty could be coordinated, and how pain could become entertainment. And he loved every second of it. I thought joining the basketball team would help, but it didn't. I was never allowed to actually be a part of it. Jack made sure of that. He made sure I never touched the ball, never took a shot, never scored a point. Every game, every practice, he did everything he could to keep me on the sidelines, to make sure I never got a real experience. My family would come to watch, and I would not play at all. I sat on the bench while he ran the floor, smooth, untouchable, everyone cheering him, while I felt invisible and worthless. Every pass I did not get, every shot I did not make, felt like a punch straight to my gut.

Jack was always there, always watching, always waiting. Every time I got close to the ball, he intercepted it, blocked it, and shoved me out of position. He did not just play. He dominated, and he did it to humiliate me. I worked harder than anyone, stayed late, practiced endlessly, but nothing mattered. He made it clear I was nothing. Every cheer for him, every high-five, every victory lap around the court, felt like fire on my chest. He was the king, and I was the shadow.

Then one day, after a game, the gym emptied faster than usual. The final buzzer had faded, leaving the air heavy and sticky. My backpack was in the locker room. I went back for it, thinking it would be a quick trip, a simple in and out. But the second I stepped inside, the room changed. He was there. Alone. Waiting. I froze. He did not speak or move at first. Just looked at me. Slowly. Patiently. Maliciously.

It was the look of someone who had been planning every second of this encounter for the entire year. My chest tightened. My legs went weak. My arms went dead. My mind screamed at me to move, to run, to do anything, but it did not respond. He stepped forward, deliberate and calm, cutting off every route of escape. My back pressed into the lockers.

The metal bit into my shoulder, cold and unyielding. My stomach sank. Every instinct told me this was wrong. Every nerve in my body screamed danger. And yet, I could not move. He raised one arm and planted his hand against the locker beside my head, boxing me in. His forearm was inches from my face. He leaned closer, and I felt his breath on my face. He grabbed my hair in the back of my head hard and tried to kiss me. I instinctively moved my head in disgust. He angrily shoved me down onto my knees. By this point, his towel fell off. He stared into my eyes and said, "You know you want this." I was still frozen, unable to move. He slowly moved himself closer to my face. I could feel the weight and heat of his body getting closer and closer. It seemed like I was in a dream, like there was no way this could be real. The locker room felt smaller, the ceiling lower. My heart was hammering in my ears. My breaths came shallow and fast. I understood in that moment that this was a real danger. Not humiliation. Not bullying. Something worse.

Time stretched. Every second felt heavier than the last. I remember thinking that if I did not move now, I never would. Something snapped. I punched him in his balls with everything I had. Both hands. All my fear. All my panic. It was clumsy and desperate, but it was enough to knock him off balance for half a second. That was all I needed.

I ran. I bolted out of the locker room, my shoes slapping against the gym floor, my lungs already burning. I heard him behind me immediately. He was faster than me. He had always been faster. On the court. In the halls. Everywhere. His footsteps were closing the distance. I knew then that I was not going to outrun him. My vision narrowed. My legs felt like they were moving through water. I remember thinking, with a strange clarity, that this was it. That I was going to die in that gym. And what scared me most was not the fear. It was how calm everything suddenly felt. Like my body had already accepted it. Then the door to the gym opened. The sound cut through everything. The basketball coach stepped inside, keys in hand, mid-stride, completely unaware of what he had just interrupted. Jack stopped instantly. The change was immediate. Like a switch had been flipped. He slowed, straightened, stepped back. Whatever had been coming collapsed in on itself. He became a different person in a fraction of a second. The coach looked at me and asked if everything was okay. He looked very confused and asked Jack why he was naked, and told him to go put some clothes on. He slowly retreated back to the locker room. Like a snake slithering back into its hole, to plot its next plan of attack. I nodded and said I was okay. I do not know how I managed it. My hands were shaking. My legs barely held me up. I grabbed my backpack, walked past the coach, and left, every muscle screaming, afraid that if I broke into a run again, I would fall apart completely. I genuinely believe the coach saved my life. Not metaphorically. Literally. One second later, and no one would have been there. I never went back to that school again. At the time, I thought that was the end of it. That leaving meant escape. That survival was enough. I was wrong. Little did I know that night was not the last time I would see Jack. And I would not have chosen how or when our paths crossed again.

After I stopped going to that school, I disappeared for a while. Not physically. Internally. That entire summer became about recomposing myself. Stitching something new together out of whatever I had left. I buried myself in punk rock. The kind that didn't ask permission. The kind that sounded like survival. I started sewing patches onto my clothes by hand. Safety pins. Torn fabric. Black mitten nail polish on fingers that were always shaking just a little. I dyed my hair platinum blond and pushed it straight up into three-inch Liberty spikes. I wore Converse All-Stars and clothes nobody would be caught dead in. Every morning felt like suiting up for battle. Every outfit was a decision. I looked like an emo kid because that's what I was. A kid trying to build an identity loud enough to drown out what had already happened to him.

By the end of the summer, I had something that looked like confidence. Or at least defiance. I mistook the two for a long time. Then school started again.

Public school. Middle of nowhere. A small hick town, Cave Junction. Cowboy boots. Trucks. Mud on tires. People who had grown up together their entire lives and knew exactly who belonged and who didn't. I didn't. That version of me I had built all summer wasn't just okay there. It was a target. I had zero friends. I couldn't even look girls in the eyes. I walked through lunch, watching faces packed tight around tables, laughing with people they'd known since kindergarten. I would make eye contact with an empty seat. I wished I could belong, and they would just look back at me "Don't you even dare." So I stopped trying. I started eating lunch in the bathroom, sitting in a stall. Knees pulled in. Listening to bells ring. Just waiting for it to be over. Going from period to period like a sentence being served. Girls eventually talked to me, but not because they liked me. Because I was nice. Because I was useful. They'd flirt just enough to get me to do their homework, then laugh about it later with their jock boyfriends while I stood there pretending not to hear.

Everyone wanted to fight me. Sometimes they didn't even bother pretending it was about anything. Two of the bigger football players cornered me in the library once. Pushed my head into a stack of books. Punched me in the stomach until I dropped to my knees. They laughed and walked away. I was hunted. They would break into my locker and fill it with tampons every day. And on top of all of that, I was poor. Really poor. Micky and Kevin had no money. I had barely any clothes. No safety net. No way out. That was when the feeling started. The tightness. The pressure. The sense that if I didn't take something, nothing was coming. That's when the stealing started.

It was small at first. A videotape. A DVD. Something easy. Something that felt harmless. Then it grew. That was when Ethan entered the picture. Ethan lived down the street. Same age. Same kind of restless energy. The kind of kid who already knew how to disappear when adults weren't looking. He wasn't loud. He was sharp. Slowly, the theft grew bigger. We got some walkie-talkies. Starting to have lookouts. Signals. We treated it like a video game. Coordinated.

Methodical. One of us watching the street. One of us inside the house. One of us ready to move. We went into the neighbors' houses and helped ourselves. Anything of value. Anything we could carry. Electronics. Cash. Small things that turned into bigger things. We hit one house and took everything we could hold. The rush was immediate. Heart pounding. Hands shaking. That moment where everything slows down and you think, am I really getting away with this? We were.

They never caught me. I was good at it. Too good. Until Kevin found out. He went door to door. Apologized. Begged. Returned everything he could. Paid cash for what he couldn't. Most of the neighbors let it go. One didn't.

That was when Kevin made the decision.

Reform school. Back to L.A. A boy's home for troubled teenagers. The neighbor agreed not to press charges if I was gone and served a one-year sentence at this home. I didn't know it then, but that was the beginning of my way back. Back home. Back to where it all started. Back to LA. And I had no idea what I was about to walk into.

5

ESCAPE FROM LA

The bus ride to Los Angeles took twenty-four hours. Seven hundred miles. By myself.

Sixteen years old. I watched everything I knew shrink through the window. Trees turning into desert. Silence turning into

noise. I didn't know if I was being sent away or brought back. All I knew was I wasn't in control anymore. Mitchell was back in LA. He was the reason I didn't end up with a record or end up in juvie. The reason my future didn't close before it even started. This was all because of him. Mitchell had ties to a church in Echo Park. A big one. Not subtle. The kind of place that took up space. One hundred thousand people every Sunday. The church ran a massive outreach program. They fed homeless people. Housed people with addictions. Ran programs most people didn't even know existed unless they needed them. One of those programs was for troubled teens. That's where I was sent.

It wasn't a facility. It wasn't a campus.

It was a house. A real house on the corner, right next to the Center. Inside it were fifteen boys. All of them more hardened than me. More experienced in things I had only seen from a distance. I was the only white kid there. Most of them were from the city. Urban. Street smart in a way I wasn't. Some were there for attempted murder. Some for gang activity. Some things nobody explained to me. Compared to them, my crime felt small. I was there for stealing. They talked in codes I didn't understand. Gang terms. Street language. Names and rules I had never learned. I nodded a lot. Stayed quiet. Tried not to stand out. I felt completely out of place. The counselor slept on a mattress at the top of the stairs every night. In the hallway right outside the bedrooms. So nobody could run. Because people always tried. Almost everyone wanted out. It felt less like a program and more like a holding cell. Almost like jail. The place ran on levels. You didn't start at the bottom, but you weren't free either. You came in on Level Two. If you behaved, you earned Level Three. More privileges. More trust. Level One meant nothing. No freedom. No extras. Just existing. That was the first phase. That house. Those boys. Those rules. That was where my life paused. Being sixteen, I hated being locked up. I didn't have the language for it then, but I felt trapped in my body. Trapped in time. Trapped in a system that decided when I could move, speak, eat, or disappear. At first, it was a house. Then the program changed ownership and everything changed with it. They moved us out of the house and into the building. A massive one. Old. Towering. The kind of place that used to be something else before people decided it could be repurposed. It looked like a sanitarium. Like an abandoned mental hospital, someone had slapped fresh paint on it and called it progress. It had endless floors. Long hallways. Locked doors. Key cards. Every floor is under renovation, but every floor is still breathing its past. You couldn't get in or out without permission. It wasn't a home. It wasn't even a school. It was a jail wearing a hospital's face. When the new ownership took over, the tone shifted immediately. It wasn't strict before. Now it was punishment. If you misspoke, you wrote sentences. Thousands of them. If you broke a rule, you lost levels. If you ran, you lost everything. Level one meant isolation. Twenty-one days. Alone in a room with nothing but a twin mattress on the floor. No clothes. No books. No distractions.

Your food was brought to you. You ate sitting on the mattress. You slept on the mattress. You stared at the walls for twenty-one days straight. I learned quickly what level one felt like. I ran, over and over again. When I ran away, I had no concept of how close I was to dying. I was sixteen. That age where you think fear is something you can outrun. Where danger still feels theoretical. I didn't understand that downtown Los Angeles isn't neutral ground. It belongs to someone, always. Block by block. Color by color. And I was walking through it like none of that applied to me. I had a skateboard under my arm and nothing else. No plan. No place to go. Just motion. The streets felt loud in a way I wasn't used to. Sirens in the distance. Cars rolling slow. People watching longer than they needed to. I stuck out immediately. White kid. Skateboard. Lost. I didn't know it yet, but I was already marked. That's when the Escalade rolled up. Black. Tinted windows. Engine idling like a warning. It stopped right beside me, close enough that I could smell exhaust and leather. The window came down just enough to reveal a man leaning toward me. There was a gun resting on his lap. Not waved. Not raised. Just there. Casual. Heavy. Real. He asked me what I was doing in his neighborhood.

I didn't even understand the question.

He accused me of tagging. Of marking walls. Of disrespecting something I didn't even know existed. His voice was flat, controlled. Not angry. Worse than angry. Certain. I tried to explain, but my words didn't sound right even to me. My mouth went dry. My hands shook. I remember staring at the barrel, thinking how small it looked for something that could erase me.

For a few seconds, I was sure that was it.

I remember thinking, this is how it ends. On a sidewalk. Over something I didn't even do. Then he really looked at me.

Not the skateboard. Not my clothes. Me.

I think he saw it immediately. The ignorance. The panic. The truth. I wasn't a threat. I wasn't a rival. I wasn't anything. Just a stupid kid who had wandered somewhere he didn't belong. He shook his head slowly. Told me to get the fuck out of there. The window went up. The Escalade rolled away. I stood there frozen, my heart slamming so hard it hurt. When my legs finally worked again, I walked fast. Didn't look back. Didn't stop. I kept walking and I ended up underground. The train station felt like another world. Fluorescent lights flickering. Concrete walls stained with years of neglect. Homeless people everywhere. Sleeping. Shouting. Fighting with ghosts that only they could see. The air smelled like piss and metal and something rotten underneath it all. I heard gunshots somewhere above me. Or close. I couldn't tell. I went deeper. Down into the subway.

That's where he came from. A homeless man pushing a shopping cart piled high with bags and trash. He wore a plastic propeller hat as if it were a joke only he understood. His mouth was empty. No teeth. Just gums and a grin that didn't match his eyes. He saw me and locked onto me. Before I could react, he grabbed me. Stronger than he looked. Hands on my arms. He tried to lift me, laughing, mumbling something I couldn't understand. The cart rattled beside us. He tried to put me in it. I realized what he was trying to do. I panicked. I kicked. Flailing. Desperate. My skateboard clattered to the ground. I felt his grip loosen for a second, and I took it. I picked up my skateboard and swung it as hard as I could into the side of his head. He fell, and he fell hard. I ran. I didn't stop until my lungs burned and my vision tunneled. That night taught me something I should have already known. I wasn't brave. I wasn't rebellious. I was lucky. I had been walking through a city that did not care if I survived. And somehow, by accident, by ignorance, by grace I didn't earn, I made it out. I didn't understand it then. But looking back now, I know how close I came to disappearing. I did this same thing over and over again. I had family in L.A.; Jennifer lived there. Jameson lived there. I didn't feel like I was escaping danger. I felt like I was running toward air. The first time I ran, I made it a few days. Then the police found me. They handcuffed me. Put me in the back of the car. Drove me to the station. Then delivered me right back to the building like a package that didn't belong anywhere else. Straight to level one. Twenty-one days. Mattress. Boxers. Nothing else. I ran again. Once to Jameson's mansion. Once to Jennifer's house. Every time, the same ending. Police. Handcuffs. Station. Back to the building. Back to the room. Back to the mattress. Over and over. Sometimes I didn't even run because I wanted freedom. Sometimes I just wanted to feel normal for a few hours. Kill Bill came out in 2003. I ran away just to see it. That's how empty my world had become. No movies. No music. No outside. No choice. Just rules, walls, and time that refused to move. I watched the movie. Then I got caught. Then I got dragged back. Again. Twenty-one more days. Boxers. Mattress. Four walls. It was worth it. That was my life. This went on for months. Running. Getting caught. Being dragged back. Twenty-one days on a mattress. Over and over. Eventually, I earned my way back to level two. That word, earned, is almost funny now.

Level two meant I could breathe again. It meant I could leave the room. It meant I was considered human enough to exist in the building rather than be stored inside it.

And through all of it, Mitchell never left.

He was there the entire time. Once a month, I was allowed to leave for a single day. One day outside. One day of air. One day that reminded me I wasn't already gone.

Mitchell always picked me up. He'd take me out to eat. Real food. He'd buy me clothes because I didn't have any. He'd take me to movies. Movies mattered to me. Jameson used to take me when I was younger. Every week. Driving me through

Beverly Hills in his Mercedes, just to sit in the dark and disappear into something bigger than my life. That stuck with me. Mitchell carried that tradition forward. Once a month was the only day I looked forward to. I knew why he was doing it. He was trying to protect my future. Trying to make sure my life didn't end before it started. And it wasn't cheap.

The program costs around five thousand a month. Mitchell paid for it out of pocket. He had a cell phone company. He had invented a type of cell tower. He had money. And he spent it on me. Quietly. Without asking for anything back.

Because of Mitchell, I still had a chance.

But every time I returned, the doors closed behind me again. Cold. Heavy. Final. That place didn't care who picked you up on the outside. Inside, it was still empty.

When I finally stabilized, they let me start going to church again. Youth group. Structure. Somewhere to sit that wasn't a mattress. That's where I saw her. She was standing across the room. Twenty feet away. And I knew instantly I loved her. She looked just like Britney Spears did in the early 2000s. The kind of beauty you don't assume belongs in your world. The kind you assume you're never meant to speak to. I thought there was no chance. Week after week, I saw her there. And week after week, I didn't say a word. Then one day, I found out she had asked about me. That she liked me. It didn't make sense. It felt impossible. Her name was Amber. We started sneaking out at night. Timing it around when the guards fell asleep. I'd climb up to the roof from my side. She'd climb up from hers. We'd lie there under the stars. Talking. Laughing. Being sixteen in a way I hadn't been allowed to be. That's where I had my first kiss. When I kissed her, everything else disappeared. The building. The rules. The levels. The doors. All of it melted away. For the first time in a long time, the world went quiet for the right reason. It was just us. On a roof. Under the stars. And for that moment, nothing else mattered. Then the summer ended. And Amber had to leave. She lived about an hour outside of L.A. Somewhere far enough that it might as well have been another world. I remember the last time I saw her. We were standing there, her hand wrapped in mine, and she was crying so hard she could barely breathe. They were calling for her to board the bus. She didn't want to let go. Neither did I. She stood there holding my hand, crying, telling me she loved me. Telling me to write her. Promising she always would. It felt unreal. Like a movie scene I didn't want to end. I didn't want her to go. I loved her.

It was the first time I had ever felt anything like that for a woman. Real. Whole. Undeniable. And just like that, she was taken from me. She let go of my hand, the tears falling down her face. Snatched away. It broke me. At the same time, I had finally made it to level three. Level three meant freedom. Privileges. Movement. Trust. It was hard to get there. Harder than anything I'd done in that place. And I had earned it. But the moment Amber left, none of it mattered. A few weeks later, I ran.

Again. I took a bus to her house. I didn't think it through. I just went. I needed to see her. Needed to know she was real. Needed to feel that moment again. Her house was big. Not a mansion, but close. Quiet. Manicured. A different world. I knocked on the door. Her parents answered. They didn't know who I was. I asked for Amber. The parents looked confused, wondering why I was there. Suddenly, I saw a boy walk into the house through the back door with Amber. His arms around her, my age. Clean. Confident. Polo shirt. Curly hair. He looked like money. Like safety. Like everything I wasn't. He looked at me and said, "Can I help you?" I said I was here for Amber.

He smiled." That's my girlfriend." She froze when she saw me, her jaw dropped like she had seen a ghost. She hadn't known I was coming. The boy turned to her. "Do you know this guy?" She didn't hesitate.

"No," she said. "I've never seen him before in my life." That was it. That was the first time, out of many, that I felt my heart break. That moment crushed me. Not loudly. Not dramatically. Just completely. It was the first time I understood heartbreak. The kind that doesn't scream. The kind that caves in. The

kind that leaves you standing there with nothing to hold onto. I didn't say anything.

I turned around and left. Walking down the driveway with tears in my eyes, feeling like nothing as I should disappear. And once again, it ended the same way it always did.

Police. Handcuffs. A ride back. Twenty-one days. On a mattress. In a room. With nothing. That was how I learned about love.

And that was how it taught me what it costs.

After they dragged me back, after the door closed again, after level one swallowed me whole, something in me snapped. I sat on that mattress for days. Boxers. Concrete. Fluorescent light that never shuts off.

I wasn't scared anymore. I was furious.

Heartbroken in a way that felt physical. Like something had been ripped out and left bleeding. I kept replaying Amber's face. His arm around her, the lie. The handcuffs. The bus. The mattress. I remember thinking, fuck this. I'm not doing this again. I started talking to the other boys. Quiet at first. Whispers through doors. Through the vents, Looks exchanged when guards weren't paying attention. Everyone had the same face. Same exhaustion. Same rage. We made a plan. There was a water station on the level. A hose. A weak point no one thought mattered. We waited. Then we moved all at once. The hose came loose. Water poured out fast. Too fast. It spread across the floor, then kept going.

Inches deep. Cold. Sloshing. Electrical hum in the walls. Chaos starting to breathe.

We filled water balloons. As many as we could. Hands shaking. Laughing in that manic way right before something explodes.

Then it happened. We rushed the guards together. Water everywhere. Balloons flying. Exploding on impact. Walls. Faces. Uniforms. The floor turned into a flooded battlefield. People slipping. Shouting. We tackled them and wanted them to feel the same pain they put on us. Alarms started to scream. I was in front, leading the charge. I don't know how that happened, but it did. I was yelling. Not words. Just sound. Just years of being trapped coming out of my throat. I remember thinking I am not sitting in that room again. Not for loving someone. Not for wanting a life. Someone threw smoke bombs. They hit the water and hissed.

Smoke rolled low across the floor. Thick. Blinding. Sirens went off. Fire alarms screaming. Red lights flashing. Water, smoke, and panic mixed together until no one knew where anyone was. It felt like a revolt. Us against the system. For a moment, it felt like freedom. That night was my seventeenth birthday. It was the last night I ever slept there. They sent me home after that, I finally successfully escaped. No ceremony. No speech. Just gone. Another bus. Another twenty-four hours. Same road in reverse. When I pulled into the station, I saw them immediately. Micky and Kevin.

They were standing there waiting. As soon as I stepped off the bus, they ran to me. Grabbed me. Held on like I might disappear again if they let go. Both of them talking at once. Laughing. Crying. "You're never leaving again," Kevin said. "We love you so much." I believed them. For the first time in a long time, I let myself believe it.

6

TEENAGE WASTELAND

WHEN I CAME BACK from Los Angeles, I was seventeen. I wasn't the same kid who had left. I didn't come back healed. I came back hardened. Something had set inside me. Something heavier, something harder. Something that showed in my face before I ever opened my mouth. I had been locked up. I had been broken down. I had learned what it felt like to lose and still stand back up. I walked differently. I carried myself differently. I went back to school. Back to the same hick high school in Cave Junction. Same hallways. Same boots. Same looks. Same people who thought they remembered who I was. They didn't. People still tried me. They still talked. Still pushed. Still tested. But I was bigger now. Taller. Six foot two. I had weight on me. I wasn't small anymore, and I wasn't scared. I joined the wrestling team. I joined the football team. And when that still wasn't enough for them, I did what came naturally. I fought. At first, it was defense. Someone stepped too close. Someone said the wrong thing. Someone thought I was still the

46

easy target I used to be. Then it became something else. People wanted turns. The hicks would come up to me in their Carhartt jackets and matching hats. Wood shop kids. Auto shop kids. They all moved in packs. Same trucks. Same accents. Same confidence that comes from never being challenged. They would circle me. Talk shit. Ask if I wanted to take it outside. I always did. One by one. Out back. No teachers. No rules. Just dirt, fists, and a crowd forming before the first punch ever landed. I didn't just fight back. I won. Every time. People would surround us. Shouting. Laughing. Cheering. Saying my name. Watching the kid who used to get hunted now stand in the middle of it, unflinching.

That was my first taste of fame. Not the good kind. Not the kind you enjoy. The kind that makes people watch you. The kind that makes people talk. The kind that makes you a story instead of a person. I never got to sit in it. Every fight ended the same way. Suspension. Days out of school. Sitting at home. Waiting. Knowing it would happen again as soon as I came back. But something had already shifted. People didn't see a victim anymore. They saw someone dangerous. And I learned something in that place. If you can't be left alone, you can at least be feared. By the time I became a senior, something had shifted again.

I wasn't popular. I wasn't loved. But I wasn't hunted the way I used to be. I had finally figured out the rhythm of survival. When to speak. When to stay quiet. When to hit back. When to walk away. I wasn't invisible

I joined the football team because I was big and thought that was enough. I didn't have money for cleats. They sent me to the loaner box. A plastic bin full of other people's leftovers. Shoes bent out of shape by feet that weren't mine. Laces frayed. Eyelets stretched. Nothing fit. I kept trying anyway. Pride does that. I finally found a pair that didn't crush my toes, but the laces were too long. I wrapped them. Tucked them. Told myself it would be fine.

It wasn't. I lined up on the field as a lineman. Helmet heavy. Breath loud inside it.

The guy across from me was bigger. Meaner. Already smiling like he knew how this would end. The ball snapped. I stepped forward, and he hit me. Hard. Clean. And when he did, my foot caught the lace.

I went down backward. The sky flipped. The field disappeared. And then there was a sound inside my body I will never forget. A crack. Sharp. Wrong. My neck snapped back farther than it was ever meant to go. White heat shot through me, and everything went quiet for a second, like the world paused to see if I was dead. I wasn't.

An ambulance came and took me away. I was a half inch from being paralyzed. I never fully recovered, it was never the same again. This was the root of future addiction, demons I had to face and overcome. Senior year, I'd never been drunk. Never been to a party. Never even been invited to one. Everyone talked about these parties out on a ranch owned by two brothers, everybody knew. Their dad was rich. Big company. Big house. Big land. The kind of place where rules didn't reach. I always heard about it after the fact. Who hooked up with who. Who fought. Who passed out. I wanted to see it once. Just once. So one night I snuck out of my house and got a ride, and just went alone. I got out and walked down this ranch driveway, not knowing what to expect at the end of it. As I approached, the ranch was lit up like a movie set. Trucks everywhere. Music spilling out into the dirt. And when I walked in, I realized something immediately. Everyone was there. The popular kids. The athletes. The girls I'd never spoken to. The guys who laughed at people like me in the hallways. I could feel it in the way the room paused when they saw me. That look. Why the hell are you here? I told the truth. I said I'd never been drunk before. That's when their faces changed. Not mean. Excited. Someone shoved a beer into my hand. Then another. Then another. I drank them because that's what you did. The taste didn't matter. And then something happened. The room softened. My chest loosened. I laughed. I talked. I felt light. For the first time in my life, I wasn't calculating every sentence before I said it. I thought this was what confidence felt like. They saw it immediately. Let's see what we can get him to do, they said. They told me brown sugar would get me drunk faster. I ate a spoonful like medicine. Paprika next. Burned my throat. Everyone laughed. Someone told me to chug water between drinks. Then they handed me an orange juice bottle, cloudy and warm. "This one's strong," they said. "The best Mixed drink." I didn't ask what was mixed. I drank it. The room exploded in laughter. I didn't understand why until someone finally told me. One of the hottest girls in school had peed in it. Mixed with alcohol. And I had just swallowed all of it without hesitation. I laughed too. I had to. Laughing felt safer than realizing I'd just been turned into a joke. They kept going. They dared me to take shots mixed with hot sauce and flat soda. Told me it would "activate" the alcohol. Had me eat salt straight out of their palms. Someone blindfolded me and told me to guess drinks that weren't drinks at all. Vinegar. Soy sauce. Something bitter and chemical I never identified. Each time, they laughed harder. Each time I felt lighter. Dumber. Easier. Eventually, I collapsed onto a couch. My body buzzing. My head floating. There was an 80s song playing on repeat. The same chorus over and over, like it was stuck in the walls. I kept fading in and out. Waking up just long enough to realize I didn't know where I was, then slipping back under. The music followed me into sleep. I woke up in the morning with the sun already high and my mouth tasting like metal and regret. I left without saying goodbye. No one stopped me. No one noticed. I never forgot that night. Not because it was fun. But because it worked. That was the first night I learned what alcohol could give me. Relief. Confidence. Silence. And I chased that feeling hard. That night wasn't a fluke. It was a blueprint. One night turned into another. And another. Each one darker. Louder. More reckless. More damaging.

That was just the beginning of a party that never stopped. As the year progressed I bought my first car. A Jeep Grand Cherokee. Old. Beat up. Almost ten years behind its time. But it was mine. It ran. It looked good enough. Better than a lot of the trucks people drove. I loved that Jeep more than I should have. It meant freedom. It meant movement. It meant I didn't have to wait on anyone. That

Jeep took me everywhere. Out past Cave Junction. Out past the pavement. Out into Tekilma. Johnny lived out there. He had a trailer in the middle of nowhere, surrounded by trees and dirt and half built hippie communes that looked like they had given up halfway through becoming something. People drifted in and out of that place. Parties. Drinking. Music. Smoke hanging heavy in the air. His trailer became a gathering point. We drank. We experimented. We disappeared for nights at a time. Mushrooms were everywhere. An eighth at a time. Sometimes night after night. No structure. No guidance. Just escape stacked on top of escape. One night, the mushrooms took me somewhere else. I remember leaving my body. Watching myself from above. Seeing myself shaking on the couch like I wasn't inside it anymore. Floating up toward the ceiling, detached, distant, weightless.

Then I heard it. Bam. Boom. Boom.

Johnny was outside hitting the side of the trailer with a bat. I snapped back into my body instantly. My heart was racing. My hands were shaking. Johnny's eyes were different that night. Wide. Intense. Quiet in a way that felt dangerous. Like something was breaking behind them, and no one was stopping it. He stepped in with the bat and smashed it onto his kitchen table, shattering it into a million pieces. As time went on, we kept going back anyway. Drinking. Mushrooms. Chaos disguised as fun. That was also the year I lost my virginity. This one cute girl was at the trailer, and I always had a crush on her. I brought her to the back of my Jeep. As it happened, all the buildup. All the hype. All the stories. I thought to myself, it's finally happening! And when it was over, it meant nothing. She went back inside. I went to sleep in a different room. It was like it never happened. That was my first lesson in sex and validation. How it promises meaning and delivers emptiness. How it makes you feel important for a moment and invisible again right after.

New Year's Eve came. Someone dared me to chug a bottle of tequila. Cheap gold tequila. I did it in about six seconds. The entire fifth. No pause. No hesitation.

After that, everything disappeared. I remember flashes. Nothing clear.

I woke up the next morning in my Jeep, parked on a random street. My mouth hurt. My face felt wrong. My head was pounding. Blood dried down my chin. My tooth had gone through my lip. My nose was broken.

Crooked to the left. It has never been the same since. The front end of my Jeep was destroyed. I didn't know what happened.

Later, I found out. Richard did it, but everyone called him Dick and boy was he one. He beat me badly. Took my Jeep. Drove it. Wrecked it. Changed the tire. Then left me unconscious on a street so I would think I had done it myself. Like a bad joke. That was just one of many nights at Johnny's place. But Johnny didn't make it out. He loved this girl. She cheated on him. Something inside him finally gave up. His story ended with a shotgun to the head. Brain matter on the wall. Silence after. That place stopped being a place after that. And I started realizing something. Everywhere I went, chaos followed. Every escape came with a price. After that, I slowed down. Not because I was healed. Because I was empty. I got a job at the only gas station for miles. A lonely place on a stretch of road that never changed. Same pumps. Same fluorescent hum. Same faces passing through every day. It sat right near the family home, surrounded by nothing. Just trees, dirt, and time that didn't move. I worked nights. I tried to fix the Jeep.

Bent metal straightened by hand. Junkyard parts. Bolts that never lined up right. I never painted it. Never finished it. The front end was always slightly off, like it had survived something it didn't want to remember. It looked like what it was. Another ghetto vehicle held together by effort and hope.

One night, I came home late. Kevin's truck was already in the driveway. His old, beat-up '85 Chevy Luv. Rusted. Loud. Mean. He had told me before not to park behind him. More than once. I was exhausted. I parked behind him anyway. I fell asleep almost instantly. Then I woke up to the sound of an engine screaming.

Not starting. Screaming. The revving wasn't normal. It wasn't accidental. It was violent. Over and over. Like someone trying to hurt something on purpose. I ran to the window. Kevin was in his truck, ramming it into my Jeep, which was behind him. Again. And again. And again. Metal collapsed in on itself. Headlights shattered. The front end I had spent weeks trying to rebuild folded like it was nothing. Each impact echoed through my chest. He was furious. Not yelling. Not cursing. Just ramming. Over and over and over. I ran outside barefoot, my heart trying to claw its way out of my ribs. Panic. Rage. Fear all colliding at once. I screamed his name. I screamed for him to stop. He didn't look at me. His eyes were empty.

Blank. Gone. Kevin had been in pain for years by then. Old back injuries. The kind that don't heal. The kind that rots

you from the inside. He could barely walk some days. The pain never stopped.

Neither did the pills. Percocet. Oxy. Anything that promised relief. Hundreds of pills were scattered across his room like a

pharmacy that had exploded. When that wasn't enough, they put a morphine pump in his stomach. Continuous morphine straight into his spine. It helped his body. It destroyed everything else. I ran toward the truck, waving my arms, screaming for him to stop. He didn't hear me. Or he didn't care.

His foot stayed on the gas. His face stayed vacant. So I did the only thing I could think of. I punched the windshield. As hard as I could. Not to hurt him. Just to make it stop.

The glass exploded under my fist. Shattered. The sound cut through the night like a gunshot. And finally, he stopped.

The engine died. Silence rushed in. He sat there for a second, hands on the wheel, staring forward as he had just woken up from something he couldn't remember.

That was it. That was who he had become.

Not a monster. A man eaten alive by pain.

A shadow of the person who raised me.

And standing there in the dark, knuckles bleeding, my Jeep crushed, my heart pounding in my ears, I understood something I hadn't before. Some people don't fall apart loudly. Some people rot quietly until everything around them breaks.

And sometimes, you're standing too close, barefoot, covered in glass, when it happens.

I stood there after it was over. The driveway was torn apart. Metal bent. Glass everywhere. The Jeep was ruined again, worse this time, like it was never meant to be fixed in the first place. Kevin's truck sat crooked and quiet, steam hissing out of it like it was breathing heavy after a fight. My hand was bleeding. Not badly. Just enough. I wiped it on my shirt and felt nothing. No shock. No regret. No adrenaline. Just stillness. That scared me more than anything else that had happened that night. I caught my reflection in the shattered windshield. Not clearly. Just pieces of my face broken across the glass. One eye here. My mouth there. The rest of

me fractured and rearranged into something new. I looked older. Not stronger. Not tougher. Just settled. For the first time, I realized I wasn't reacting anymore. I wasn't panicking. I wasn't trying to survive the moment. I was standing inside it, calm, watching it happen like I already knew how it would end. And that's when it hit me.

I wasn't afraid of violence anymore. I wasn't afraid of breaking things. Or being broken.

Or crossing lines I used to swear I never would. I turned away from the glass and walked back inside the house. Kevin was quiet now. The pain had taken him somewhere else. Somewhere unreachable. I didn't hate him. I understood him. That was worse. I lay down fully dressed on my bed and stared at the ceiling. No shaking.

No tears. No thoughts chasing each other in circles. Just one clear realization settling into place. This is who I am now. And I didn't look away.

7

A GOD NAMED DUSTY

When I was twenty, I started going to the gym like it was a second job. Not because I loved it. Because I needed somewhere to put the damage. That was when I noticed Dusty. He was always there. Not loud. Not trying. Just present. When he walked in, the room reacted before anyone decided to look. Conversations slowed. Eyes followed. It was instinct. He looked unreal. Muscle stacked perfectly, not bulky, not showy. Huge arms that looked earned. Abs cut deep enough to look permanent. Thick hair that sat right without effort. The kind of body that made comparison feel pointless.

He looked like someone designed, not raised. He looked like an Abercrombie model that stepped out of a page into real life. Everyone wanted to be him. Nobody ever was. He existed alone in his category. I did not want him. I did not want his life. I wanted to understand what it felt like to move through the world without flinching. At that time, I did not. Years of being torn down had hollowed me out early. I did not feel attractive. I did not feel confident. Talking to women felt like standing exposed. So I lifted. And I watched. Months passed. He stayed the same. Same presence. Same gravity. Then I started working at Blockbuster. Right next door was a Dutch Bros coffee stand. Bright. Busy. Always moving. One night after my shift, I walked over for coffee. Still in my uniform. Still invisible. And there he was. A barista. Smiling. Handing out drinks like it was nothing. We talked. Just normal conversation. Gym. Work. Life.

And then we kept talking. We became friends fast. Real friends. Best friends, even, and eventually brothers. The kind that falls into rhythm without effort. What I did not know then was that I was stepping into the beginning of a decade. A stretch of years marked by movement, risk, nights that bled into mornings, and choices that would leave marks. I did not know that his presence would start shaping the outline of who I wanted to become. Not him exactly. But what he represented. The calm. The certainty. The way he carried himself without apology. It reminded me of Jameson. My grandfather had the same quiet gravity. Not loud. Not chasing attention. Just solid. Just there. A man who knew who he was and did not need the room to agree. Dusty was the first time I saw that energy in someone my own age. And once you see it, you start chasing it. Not in others. In yourself. That was the beginning. That was when the adventures started. Me and Dusty began driving to Medford, an hour away, because that is where the parties were and because cheap alcohol always lived farther from home. We were broke. No money. No plan. Just momentum.

We bought what we could afford. Orange MD 20/20 bottles that burned going down and burned again coming back up. Steel Reserve forties sweating through paper bags, Four Lokos that we could barely stomach. By the time we arrived, the night already felt loud. Word spread fast. Mostly because Dusty existed there. People noticed him first, then noticed me because I was standing next to him. Everyone wanted to be him. I was just close enough to catch the fallout. Music rattled the walls. Bodies packed into rooms not built for that many people. The air smelled like alcohol, perfume, sweat, and something electrical. Time stopped behaving normally. I stopped thinking about myself. I started becoming someone else. At a house party one night. I remember sitting on a couch next to a girl wearing a Viva La Bam shirt. Her knee brushed mine. Her hair smelled sweet and synthetic. We were talking about nothing. Laughing at nothing. Then the room shifted. The next thing I knew, we were in a bedroom with the door half closed and the music bleeding through the walls. Her shirt was gone. Suddenly, she was naked on top of me, and my hands were shaking as I took off her pants, her bra, and everything else. Everything felt fast and slow at the same time as she climbed onto me. There was a knock. Dusty cracked the door open just enough to smirk. He tossed a condom into the room without ceremony. Are you done yet? The door shut with a laugh. The music swallowed us again. That was the tone. Another night. Another house. Same chaos, different walls, different girls, but the same outcome. Billy was always there. Always hovering. Watching everything we did felt like a show. I ended up with two girls the next weekend. One skinny, her braces flashing every time she laughed, long brown hair falling into her face. The other blonde, taller, softer, still lean but fuller than the first. They followed me down the hallway without asking questions. The room was small. The light was low. Everything blurred into skin, breath, movement. Hands everywhere. All our clothes were thrown onto the floor. Laughter turning into something heavier. I quickly learned how to handle two women at once. Time collapsed completely. At one point, I noticed the window. Dusty and Billy were outside, standing in the dark, watching through the glass like it was a movie they had already seen once and wanted to watch again. Dusty nodded, almost approving. Billy just stared in shock as I made both of them orgasm at the exact same time. I did not feel embarrassed. I felt hollowed out and powerful at the same time each time they moaned my name. That became the pattern. Parties. Sex. Being known for things I never planned to be known for. Moving through rooms like nothing could touch me. Borrowing Dusty's gravity and letting it carry me places, I did not stop to question. I thought I was becoming someone. I did not realize yet what it was costing me. One night we went to Ashland. Dusty, Billy, and I. The dorms were massive. Concrete stacked on concrete. Windows lit up like a hive. Thousands of people living on top of each other. Noise everywhere. Laughter bleeding down stairwells. Music echoing through courtyards. We drifted into a small dorm room party. Nothing special. Just bodies and beer. Low ceilings. Too many people. The kind of place where the air already feels used. I heard it before I noticed it. Girls whispering behind us. That tone.

Oh my god. That is him. That is him.

I did not turn around. None of us did. You learn early not to acknowledge it. Attention is a spark. You never know what it lights. A big football-looking guy appeared at the door. Big. Red-faced. Veins out. He started screaming. Not words at first. Just sound. Raw and furious. He was not even aiming it at one of us. Just unloading it into the room like a bomb. We did not argue. We walked out, we left. The night air hit cold and sharp as we walked outside. For half a second, I thought that was it. We made it out safe, then the door behind us burst open. He followed us outside. And so did everyone else. Twenty-five. Thirty guys at least. Football players. Track guys. Thick necks. Wide shoulders. The kind of bodies that move together. They fanned out fast and closed the circle without thinking. We were trapped, surrounded. Hundreds of people poured out of the dorms. Windows filled. Balconies stacked with faces. Phones out. Everyone watching like it was entertainment. The screaming locked onto Billy. That was when we found out. The football player's Sister. Pregnant. Abortion. Refused Money. Rage. The football player was inches from Billy's face. Spit flying. Threats stacking. Killing us. Beating us.

Leaving us there. I could feel my heartbeat in my throat. My hands were cold. My legs felt too light. The circle around us pressed tighter. No gaps. No exits. Just muscle, anger and breath. I started talking. I do not remember what I said. Apologies. Calm words. Reason. Anything that might slow it down. I kept my voice low and steady like that mattered. Like it could reach him. It did not. The crowd leaned in. I saw Billy's face, he started smiling, unfazed by the gorilla screaming into his face. Then he reached into his pocket. I saw it before I understood it. A flare gun. He raised his hand upwards, slowly and confidently. He fired it straight up. The sky exploded red. Light flooded the courtyard. Smoke burned the air. People screamed and flinched back. The circle broke just enough. We ran. No direction. Just away. We heard Footsteps behind us. Shouting. Adrenaline ripping through my chest. I thought I felt hands grab at my jacket. I thought this was how it ended. Then sirens. Security lights flooded the grass. Radios crackled. The chase slowed. The crowd stalled. The football players peeled back toward the dorms, trying to make sense of what just happened. We did not stop running until our lungs burned. When we finally slowed down, my hands were shaking so hard I had to sit down. Nobody said anything. The night went quiet again, like it always does after something almost happens. That was the pattern, too. Chaos. Close calls. Moments where everything could have ended and did not. Me and Dusty ran wild. That was the nature of it—chaos, motion, inside jokes that crossed lines. We were best friends in the way people are when they mistake intensity for loyalty. We loved each other, but we loved testing each other more. We fucked with each other constantly. He liked to fuck with women also; it was his favorite. One time we're at this girl's house, she was giving him a blow job. When he finished, he finished strong on a piece of bread. Afterward, he made her eat it; she was forever known as "wonder-bread" from then on. One night, I was in Medford, an hour away, on a date with a girl whose name I do not remember—movie theater parking lot. The popcorn smell is still clinging to my clothes. I walked out, got into my car, and turned the key. Nothing. My car was a piece of shit. A 1994 Geo Storm. Three-cylinder hatchback. Barely louder than a lawnmower. Sixty miles a gallon if you treated it right. I popped the hood and leaned in. All the spark plugs were unplugged. I did not hesitate. I knew it was Dusty. That was his kind of joke. Quiet. Surgical. Just enough to ruin your night.

I drove home pissed but smiling. When I got home, I grabbed a plastic bag. Scooped dog shit off the ground. I walked down the street to Dusty's place. His truck was parked out front. Big. Clean. Proud. I smeared it into the tailgate slowly, deliberately, the gloves squeaking faintly as I pressed my hand against the metal. I wrote a message. "I'm watching you." I left without knocking. The next day, the story came back to me sideways. Dusty laughed at first. Then he did what Dusty always did when he felt cornered. He escalated past humor. He told someone he was going to kidnap my little brother, Kasey, who was five. Maybe six. He did not mean it. That was obvious to me. But intent does not matter once words leave your mouth.

The wrong people heard. Micky despised Dusty from the beginning. She said there was nothing in his eyes. An empty soul. A sickness. She said he was a narcissist. A sociopath. She said she could feel it. Kevin heard the kidnapping comment. Kevin did not laugh. Kevin was already unraveling then. This was after the farm. After things had started shifting in him. He was holding himself together with rage by a thread.

He went to Dusty's house with a crossbow.

Kevin stood on Dusty's porch, pounding on the door, crossbow in his hands. Face red. Screaming obscenities. "Open the door. Open the fucking door. You want to threaten my son." Dusty did not open it.

For the first time, he did not have a move. He did not joke. He did not posture. He froze. He called the cops. Red and blue lights washed over the house. The crossbow was taken. Kevin was taken in with it. Dusty stood there shaking. Silent. Smaller than anyone had ever seen him. That was the moment the line stopped being blurry. What started as chaos turned into consequence. What felt like games started pulling in people who did not belong in them. Kids. Cops. Weapons. Kevin never fully came back from that period. That night was just one crack in a series of cracks that started and never really closed. What stayed with me was not the yelling or the lights. It was the realization that the games were no longer contained to us. They had started spilling outward.

And once that happens, the ending is already in motion. By then, the partying wasn't accidental anymore. It was scheduled. Medford had a rhythm, and I learned it fast. Thursday nights meant faces I recognized. Friday meant people I didn't. Saturday meant nothing mattered. Every weekend followed the same map, and I stopped pretending I wasn't following it on purpose. I was inside the crowd now.

Not watching it. Not borrowing it. Inside it.

It always started on Thursday nights. Open mic. Low lights that made everyone look better than they were. Sticky floors that caught your shoes when you shifted your weight too fast. The hum of amps warming up. People waiting their turn to be heard, pretending that was the reason they showed up. It wasn't. There were women everywhere. Not romance. Not dating. Availability. Bodies packed close enough that heat carried. Knees brushing.

Hands landing where they didn't need to land and staying there just long enough to mean something. Everyone looking. Everyone pretending they weren't. Alcohol softened the edges. Coke sharpened them again. Time stopped behaving like time.

I had learned how to move by then.

How to stand still and let attention come to me. How to hold eye contact without smiling. How to speak slowly enough that people leaned in. I didn't chase anymore. I waited. I could feel myself changing. I wasn't Dusty. I wasn't Jameson. But I was stitching pieces of both together. The calm. The presence. The confidence that didn't ask permission and didn't explain itself. It felt like becoming something. After the sets ended and the room loosened, the night spilled outward. People drifted into the parking garage across the street. Concrete ramps. Cold air hitting hot skin. The sound of laughter echoing too loud off cement walls. That's where things happened fast.

Women followed me down those ramps like gravity had shifted. Into my little Geo Storm at the bottom, I slept with more women than I can count in the backseat of that car. A car so small it felt like a joke. Fogged windows. Knees pressed hard against them. Breath breaking breathing so loud that we were both wet with sweat by the end. I went into a bar like I was fishing, put out a line, see who bit and then I would take her out to my car and have sex with her. I don't know how it worked. I don't know why it did. I just know it kept happening. Over and over. Different faces. Same hunger. Same motion. Sex without names. Without context. Without aftermath. Shirts back on. Hands wiped clean. Walking back up the ramp like nothing had happened back into the bar just to do it again. That was the pattern. Thursday warmed me up. Friday blew it open. Saturday erased it completely.

Clubs. House parties. Raves, Strangers' bathrooms. Back rooms that smelled like weed, coke mixed with something burnt. Drugs traded without counting. Bodies colliding. Pleasure that hit hard and

disappeared just as fast. Danger started to feel normal. And through all of it, Dusty never left my side. One night, New Year's Eve, it reached a scale I hadn't seen before.

The biggest party of the year. A house so packed it felt like it might collapse under the weight of bodies. Six hundred, maybe a thousand people pressed into something meant for a family. Music bleeding through walls. Floors vibrating. Alcohol sloshing out of cups faster than anyone could drink it. The night felt limitless.

Girls everywhere. Skin everywhere. Heat rising off bodies like steam. I barely remember how I met the first girl I latched onto. Faces blurred. Names lost immediately. It didn't matter. I disappeared behind the house with one of them.

Cold siding against my back. Her breath hot against my neck. The sound of the party muffled and distant like it wasn't even real. It was fast. Urgent. Animal. I lifted her up against a wall as she softly moaned into my ear. I put my hand around her throat. I ripped off her panties fast and put it in slow, then faster, and faster, she screamed my name as we both finished. It was over before either of us knew it had really started. When I came back around the corner, I wasn't even catching my breath yet when the owner of the house found me. He smiled like he already knew what was going to happen. He pulled me down a hallway and into the master bedroom, which felt detached from reality. Two girls were already there, waiting. Naked. He did not stay. He just said, "You're welcome." He closed the door and left. One of them was smaller, with dark hair falling into her face, small pale breasts. The other was taller, blonde, big fake breasts filling the room without trying. They slowly started kissing each other and both of them took off my pants like they were starving. This was the kind of sex that doesn't feel intimate so much as surreal. Like it's happening to someone else. It didn't feel earned. It felt endless. I didn't want it to end. I didn't know where I started and they began. A sea of flesh, orgasms, shrieking, over and over again. When it was over, they both got dressed and held each other as they limped out of the room. When I finally stepped back out into the night, the cold slapped me awake. Dusty was in a hot tub. Steam rose around him like smoke. A girl sat close, naked, impossibly beautiful, the kind of face that men dream of. Her head rested in his lap between his legs. She went at it like she was starving. He looked untouchable. Untethered, like a God in the pale moonlight. Like nothing bad could reach him. They all had been doing coke all night by then. Little lines passed hand to hand. Energy spiking. Heart racing. Everything is sharper, louder, and faster than it should be. That's when the sound cut through the music. Gunshots. At first, no one reacted. Then everything happened at once.

People screamed. Bodies surged toward the front of the house. I ran with them. Out on the street Someone was yelling about drugs. About Coke. A gun was raised, shaking in someone's hand, pressed inches from another man's face. Then someone shoved him onto the ground. The man with the gun jumped into his car; the engine screamed. The car lunged forward. I watched a tire roll over the man's face on the ground. Bone. Skin. Blood. The sound of it snapping through the air like something breaking inside me. The car peeled out and disappeared. I ran. Blocks away. Hands shaking. Heart hammering so hard it felt like it might crack my ribs. I got to my car and jammed the key into the door. Frozen. I twisted harder. The key snapped. I sat there in the dark, breath coming too fast, nose burning, hands shaking, convinced I had just watched someone die. The party felt a lifetime away. The road felt endless. I was an hour from home with no way to move. I called Kevin at three in the morning. He didn't ask questions. He drove a hour and showed up with the spare key. Silent. Angry in that way that meant he cared, but didn't know how to say it. He followed me the entire way home, headlights locked behind me like an anchor. That night didn't end with fireworks. It ended with me realizing how thin the line was between chaos and consequence. And how close I had been standing to it the whole time. Another night with Dusty, the biggest club in town. I was twenty. Not even close to twenty-one. I had tried to get in so many times that the bouncers already knew my face. Same result every time. A shake of the head. Go home. Dusty was twenty-one.

We walked up together like it was nothing. He handed over his ID. They leaned in, checked it, and nodded. I stayed tight to his shoulder, heart pounding, eyes forward. When they waved him through, I followed him without slowing down. Nobody stopped me. One step past the door and the sound hit like a wall. Bass shaking the floor. The lights were strobing so hard that it felt like time was skipping. A thousand bodies packed together, "Ground Zero" was what it was called, moving as one organism. Three levels of balconies stacked above the dance floor like stadium seating. I had never seen anything like it. People disappeared up there. Couples. Groups. People who didn't come back down for a long time. All having sex on the top levels. Everyone knew what happened on those balconies. Nobody pretended otherwise. It felt unreal. Like stepping into a movie I wasn't supposed to be in. They were playing everything from the 2008 era. Flo Rida. Boots with the Fur. Songs that turned the whole room into motion. Sweat. Skin. Hands sliding where they shouldn't. Dusty was already amped. He had that look in his eyes, the one that Micky talked about. The one that meant he was bored and looking to feel alive. It didn't take long. It started over a girl. Ashley. Someone I had slept with. Someone Dusty decided to start a fight with her new boyfriend. Words turned into shoves. Shoves turned into space opening up around them. The music cut. That's when you know something bad is about to happen. Everyone stopped moving. A thousand people watching two men square off under flashing lights. He pushed Dusty hard enough to make the crowd react.

Dusty didn't step back. He leaned into him and head-butted him, just like that. This dude dropped. Blood everywhere, all over his face. Security swarmed. He was dragged out limp, his night over in seconds. The music came back on like nothing had happened. I didn't even have time to process it before I felt eyes on me. On the Third balcony. An older woman. Late thirties, maybe. She hadn't stopped looking all night. Not curious. Intent. Like she had already decided she wanted me. She came down, leaned close, said my name like she already knew it. She asked if I wanted her. I said yes. We didn't talk after that. Outside, the air was cold enough to cut through the heat still clinging to my skin. We ended up in my car, bodies close, windows fogging, the club still thumping in the distance like a heartbeat. It was happening fast. I took off her pants and put my head between her legs. I climbed on top of her, the car started shaking violently from side to side. Then a bang. A Flashlight through the window. The Police. They opened the door, and the officer leaned in and asked her if she knew me. She smiled and said that I was her boyfriend and that she was drunk. That everything was fine. I asked if he could give us a minute because I wasn't finished yet. He didn't laugh. He made us get dressed, and they let us go. When we walked back toward the club, we went inside and then up to the third-floor balcony. I bent her over the railing overlooking the entire climb below us. I moved her panties to the side and put myself back in her. The cops were not going to ruin this for me. I finished in front of the entire club underneath us; it didn't even faze me. This was my first experience of power through sex. I felt untouchable. I felt like a God. After I was done, the cops came back. The music stopped. I thought they were there for me, but I realized why they were really there. They were looking for Dusty for knocking the guy out in the middle of the dance floor. He had already vanished. I found him three blocks away, breathing hard, adrenaline still humming under his skin. We laughed like idiots on the drive home, as nothing had almost gone wrong. Violence. Sex. Drugs. Alcohol. Another night where it felt like I was finding myself. Another night when I didn't realize how close I was to losing it. We laughed about it all as if it were funny. A joke only we were involved in. No one could touch us.

8

BLEED FOR ME

Meadow didn't arrive with noise.

She didn't enter rooms the way the others did. No gravity shift. No heads turning. No performance. She was already there when you noticed her, sitting on the floor, leaning against a wall, watching everything without needing to be seen. That was the difference.

By the time Meadow became part of my life, the world around me was already loud. She was blonde, short, petite, with large breasts that didn't make sense with her tiny body. She looked like someone on the cover of a Sports Illustrated bikini edition. She became a part of houses that never slept. Bodies in and out. Sex and drugs and nights that blurred so badly, mornings felt unreal. She existed outside of that current. We met in the middle of chaos, but she never belonged to it. Not the way the rest of us did. She didn't need attention to feel real. She didn't hunt it or hide from it. She moved through rooms quietly, like she understood something the rest of us hadn't learned yet.

She became my best friend without either of us deciding it. One night, we were talking on the floor while people danced over us. Another night, we were sitting outside, sharing cigarettes, listening to laughter spill out of the house like static. Then suddenly she was everywhere in my life. Not attached to me. Not orbiting me. Just present. It wasn't sexual. That mattered.

In a world where everything touched everything else, she didn't. A few drunk kisses that never meant anything. Moments that never crossed the line. She was my sister in everything but blood. The only person in that house who knew what I was thinking before I said it. She saw me without wanting anything from me.

That was rare. When I brought the girls home, she noticed before I did. Different shoes by the door. Different purses on the table. She would roll her eyes and smile, like she already knew how the night ended. She never judged me. Never praised me. Just observed. Sometimes we would lie awake in different rooms, texting while the party roared on. Talking about nothing. Talking about everything. The kind of conversations that feel insignificant until you realize they are the only honest ones you're having. She knew when I was lying to myself. She didn't call it out. She didn't try to fix it. She just stayed close enough that I couldn't fully disappear. That made her dangerous in a different way. Because when you are surrounded by chaos, the quiet becomes the loudest thing in the room. Around that same time, Dusty began to fade. Not out of my life. Out of the night.

He got a girlfriend. Madison. A real one. Something solid enough to pull him toward stability. He stopped going out. Stopped drifting from house to house. We were still brothers, but the rhythm broke. He had somewhere to be now. Someone waiting.

I didn't. So I left. I moved out of my family's place in the middle of nowhere and drove over an hour away to Ashland. Twenty years old. Almost twenty-one. First time on my own. No safety net. No rules. Just distance. The house I landed in didn't feel like a home. It felt like a crossroads. Always full. Always loud. Always on the verge of something tipping. People came and went without explanation. Nights stacked on top of each other until time stopped making sense. It was the kind of place that amplified whatever you brought into it. The first one I met was Mango. That wasn't his real name, but it fit. He moved like money. Quiet confidence. Soft voice. Expensive taste without needing to explain it. His dad had money. Real money. The house showed it. Clean lines. Good furniture. Nothing accidental. Mango lived inside ideas. Film ideas. Production ideas. Always talking about a movie he was making. Some independent project that never seemed finished. Cameras came and went. Crew rotated through. So did women. Naked women, half-dressed women, women who stayed the night and vanished by morning. The house always smelled like smoke, perfume, and ambition. Then there was Fletch. Fletch was simpler. He walked the town like it was a slot machine. Seeing what would fall into his hands. Drugs. Stories. Trouble. He was likable in a way that didn't ask permission. Everyone knew him. Everyone waved. He didn't plan much. He just moved. I believed Fletch and Mango were secret lovers, because I would always catch them leaving each other's rooms in the morning. Brandon was always there, too. Cigarettes never left his hand. American Spirits. One after another. I smoked like him by then.

Like Dusty. It had crept into me through years of parties and long nights. Brandon looked like Brad Pitt's kid. Not a joke. Same face. Same bone structure. He showed me clips from movies he'd been in. Said he was in talks to play Brad Pitt's son in a movie. I believed him. The way he carried himself made it easy to. Then there was Ramirez. Older. Thirties. Tried to act like he had class but didn't. Bald. Bitter. Always watching. Always measuring. He didn't belong there, and he knew it—the kind of guy you'd avoid in a dark alley without knowing why. I didn't like him the moment I saw him. As we settled into Ashland, Meadow started being around more and more. The house pulled people in, but she stayed. Sitting on the counter. Sitting on the couch. Sitting on the floor while the rest of us moved around her like noise. Ramirez noticed. He had a crush on her. A real one. Heavy. Uncomfortable. The kind that doesn't ask permission and doesn't understand silence. He hovered. Watched. Lingered too long when she spoke. Everyone could feel it. One afternoon, Meadow said, almost joking, "What the heck? I'll go get a cup of coffee." She went with Ramirez. When she came back, she found me first. She was blunt. Almost offended by the whole thing. She said she didn't like him. Said he wasn't attractive. Said he smelled like cheese. Dirt all over his face. Under his fingernails. Like he hadn't washed in days, she said she didn't even want to kiss him when he tried. Said his breath smelled like goat shit. She laughed when she said it. Not long after that, Meadow started dating the guy who lived next door. He had this gangster swagger that never quite fit Ashland. Jerseys. Cadillac. Gold tooth. Loud confidence. I didn't like him. Didn't trust him. But it wasn't my place. Ramirez found out. That's when something in him snapped. He came over unannounced, walked straight into the house, like he owned it. Meadow was there. He started yelling at her. Voice cracking. Eyes wild. And then, out of nowhere, he started hitting himself. Hard. Over and over. Fist to face. Smacking his own cheekbone, his mouth, his forehead. Meadow froze. She didn't know what to do. None of us did.

Then he turned on her. He lunged. Reached for her. I was walking out of the kitchen with a large bowl of hot soup in my hands. Still steaming. I didn't think. There was no pause. Just instinct. Like a reflex, I lunged the soup forward, right into his face. The soup went everywhere. He screamed.

I dropped the bowl and grabbed him. He was wearing overalls with no shirt underneath. His skin was slick with sweat and scalding soup. He smelled like cow shit. Like dirt and rot and something animal. I grabbed him by the front of his overalls and dragged him across the floor.

I threw him out of the house. Hard. I said in a calm, stoic voice, "If you come here again, I will break your legs." The door slammed behind him. He stood there for a second, screaming, face red and blistering, eyes full of something broken, filled with rage. Then he left. We never saw him again. The house went quiet. Meadow was shaking. That was the moment things changed. Not loudly. Not all at once. But something cracked.

And nothing that came after would be separate from it. After a year or two, Meadow stopped coming around as much. At first, it was barely noticeable. A missed night. A weekend, she didn't show. Then longer gaps. She started spending more time at the neighbor's house. Then, almost all of her time. I saw less of her.

Then less. Then almost nothing. When she did come back around, something was off.

A bruise on her face, half hidden under makeup. A mark on her leg, she tried to laugh away. She told stories too fast. Changed subjects. I caught it anyway. It was subtle at first. Then it wasn't. Every time I saw her, it was worse. One night I waited. I walked over to the neighbor's house. The one she was dating. I didn't plan it. I just went. I banged on the door hard enough that it rattled. He answered, holding a loaded shotgun. Short barrel. Snub-nosed. Silver. Already in his hands, like he had been waiting for a reason.

He pointed it straight at my chest.

For a split second, everything went silent.

Then Meadow ran to the door. She knocked the barrel upward just as it fired. The blast went off above me. The sound ripped through the night. My ears rang. My legs locked. I realized a half second later that I had almost been shot. She screamed. He yelled. Earlier that same day, she had told me she was excited. She had just bought a bag. Cocaine. She said it was the last one. Said she was going to rehab after. Said she was done. Said this was it. After the gun went off, she didn't look back at me. I stood there stunned. Tears in my eyes. I loved her like a sister. There was nothing I could do to save her. I knew it in that moment. That was the last time I ever saw her. The next morning, there were ambulances outside the house. Sirens. Lights. People standing in the street.

They had both overdosed and died. Found cold, naked, and blue. That was my first real loss. After that, I didn't recover. Not really. I had been there for years by then, and something inside me shut down. I started drifting back home slowly, like gravity pulling me in reverse. And I had no idea what was waiting for me there. Before I made my way home, one lonely night. In a bar, I remember being angry, heartbroken, wishing I could just see Meadow's smile just one more time. When I walked in, I knew it was him before he turned around. It didn't matter that it had been 10 years; I knew. Same laugh. Same need to be seen. Jack. I stepped up beside him at the bar. Didn't say a word. He felt it before he saw me. That instinct people get when something heavier enters the room. He turned, smile already loading, then stopped when he realized how far he had to look up. The smile didn't finish forming. "Oh," he said. I looked at him. Nothing else. He tried to laugh it off. "Damn. It's been" I didn't respond. I just stood there. The space between us stretched. The noise around us softened. Someone behind him shifted. Jack swallowed. "You good?" he asked. I tilted my head slightly. Slow. Measured. His shoulders tightened. A few seconds passed. Enough for people to notice. Enough for him to feel it. "You remember," I said. Two words. His face flushed. "Yeah, man. Of course." I let my eyes move over him. Not threatening. Not rushed. Just taking inventory. I could feel the room watching now.

I just stared at him with a look that could cut glass.

Jack laughed, but it cracked. "What's your problem?" I leaned in just enough. "You," I said quietly. I stepped back and said nothing else. That was the worst part. He started filling the silence himself. "Look," he said, louder now. "If this is about high school or some dumb shit," I raised one hand. Not aggressive. Final. He stopped mid-sentence. Fear in his eyes. Someone near the bar muttered, "Oh shit." Jack's eyes flicked around. He could see it happening. The recalibration. The way people were no longer on his side. "You should relax," he said. "You're making a scene." I smiled once, and that scared him even more. I had at least 80 pounds on him and was a whole head taller. His hands started moving. Jacket. Pockets. Face. "Man, you're acting crazy." I shook my head. He knew what was coming. Jack took a step back. "I'm leaving," he said. He turned. I grabbed him by his ear and pulled him back hard enough that the room gasped. He stumbled. I didn't rush it; I took my time. I looked him in the eye. "This," I said quietly, "is what it feels like." Then I hit him. Once. Hard. Teeth flew out of his mouth. He dropped like the floor had been waiting for him. The bar erupted behind me, but I was already stepping back. People shouting. Someone screaming his name. Chairs scraping. I looked down at him lying there, gasping, helpless, exactly how he made me feel every day of my adolescence. Feeling justified for murdering the innocent kid I used to be. Nothing left to say. I straightened, adjusted my sleeve, and walked out. No one stopped me. No one followed. Behind me, the room buzzed with shock, the kind of reaction that comes after something irreversible had happened. That was the last night I was in Ashland, then I made my way home.

9

REST IN PIECES

When I left Ashland, I didn't rush. I drifted. Back down familiar roads. Back toward the house in the middle of nowhere. Back to Micky and Kevin. Back to the place that was supposed to still be standing. I didn't know what had been happening while I was gone. I assumed time had frozen without me. It hadn't. They had been unraveling slowly. Quietly. The way people do when no one is watching close enough. Fighting. Breaking up. Getting back together. Repeating the same arguments until they stopped sounding like arguments at all. They had moved into separate rooms. That alone should have told me everything. I came back after Meadow's death, carrying pieces I didn't know how to hold. Grief. Guilt. Shock. I was trying to put myself back together, and instead I walked straight into something already breaking apart. The house felt different the second I stepped inside. Colder. Not temperature. Presence.

Kevin was restless. Always pacing. Talking about leaving. Talking about L.A. as if it were a lifeboat. Talking about moving back in with his brother, like it was the only thing left that made sense now. He had started selling his tools. All of them. Auto tools he had collected over the decades. Things that used to define him. Wrenches. Car jacks, equipment that had once meant work and pride. He laid them out like inventory. Trying to scrape together gas money to get back to L.A. Every tool sold felt like a piece of him disappearing. Micky had gone somewhere else entirely. She lived inside the computer. World of Warcraft. That was her world now. Day and night. The glow of the screen lit her face while everything else faded into background noise. She played while Kevin packed. She played while the house cracked. She played while I sat there trying to understand how this had happened without me noticing. That's where she met him. Gideon. Online. Through the game. He was 19 years old. Five years younger than me. While Kevin was planning his exit, Micky had already replaced the space. A new voice in her headphones. A new presence. Someone who hadn't seen the damage yet. Someone who only knew her through an avatar. The contrast was surreal. Kevin selling his past. Micky building a new one. I was standing in the middle of it. I didn't understand the timing then. I didn't see how close everything was to the edge. I just knew something was wrong in a way that couldn't be fixed by conversation or time. There was tension everywhere. In the walls. In the silence.

In the way no one looked at each other for too long. Kevin was leaving. Micky was elsewhere. And I had just come back. None of us were moving in the same direction anymore. I didn't know it yet, but this wasn't a rough patch. It was the beginning of the end. And it was going to end violently. Then the unthinkable happened. Kevin died. The last time I saw Kevin, I went into his room. It was quiet. Dim. I stood there for a second before I spoke. "I love you," I said. He looked at me and smiled, tired but soft. "I love you, son," I remember the last thing I ever said to him. I told him I was making a fried egg sandwich. Asked if he wanted one.

He shook his head. "No, I'm okay." That was it. Nothing dramatic. Nothing heavy. Just an ordinary moment pretending it would be followed by another one. The night before, he had taken pills. Too many. More than I had ever seen him take before. To this day, I don't know if it was an accident or a decision he made on purpose. I don't know if his hand slipped or if his mind finally gave out. I don't know if it was the pain in his back that never stopped screaming, or the pain in his chest from feeling replaced. From watching Micky move on with a 19-year-old she met online while he was still breaking apart in the same house. I don't know if he meant to go. I only know that the next day, he was in the hospital. ICU. Machines everywhere. Tubes down his throat. His body still there, but something essential already gone. I stood next to the bed and watched his chest rise and fall for him. Watched a man who had lived in pain for years finally look calm. Peaceful. For the first time. That's how I remember him now. Not angry. Not broken. Not ramming trucks or drowning in pills. Just still. At peace. That was the last time I ever saw him. And then he was gone, just like that. After that, I couldn't stay in the house. The walls held too much. Every room felt like a memory waiting to ambush me. His absence was louder than anything he had ever said. I packed what I could and left. I moved back to Medford. I took whatever work I could get. Waiting tables. Odd jobs. Anything that paid enough to keep me moving. I rented rooms from strangers on Craigslist. Slept in places that never felt like mine. Lived out of bags. Avoided stillness. Because if I stopped, I felt him. He meant too much. And suddenly, he was nowhere. Some losses don't explode.

They just hollow everything out. And you spend years learning how to live around the empty space where someone used to be.

While I was gone, I didn't see it happen. I only heard about it. Within a few months of Kevin's death, Micky moved Gideon into the house. A boy from South Carolina, 5 years younger than me, from across the country. Someone she had never met in person. She brought him straight into the home we had lived in. The same house. The same walls. The same rooms that still smelled like Kevin. She did with Gideon what she had done with Kevin. They weren't allowed to sleep in the same room. No intimacy. No touching. Nothing until marriage. Religion wrapped around everything. Gideon moved straight into Kevin's room, like he had never been there. A few months after that, just like that, they were married. That's how fast it happened. I heard this and felt something open up in me. Not grief this time. Anger. Shock. A disbelief so sharp it felt unreal. Like the story had to be wrong because no one could actually do that.

But it wasn't wrong. Karl and Kasey still lived there. Out of nowhere, Gideon started writing love letters. Not subtle ones. Not confused messages. Love letters. To one of my little underage brothers. They told someone. Word spread. Micky took Gideon's side. That was the moment everything fractured. Gideon was accused of what he did. And for a moment, it seemed like consequences might not exist. He was no longer allowed to live in the house. But Micky stayed with him. She got him an apartment. She paid for it herself. She defended him. Even after the letters. She said he didn't do it. But he had. And everyone knew it. That was the final break. The last thread snapped. The house didn't just lose people. It lost gravity. Nothing held anymore. Everything scattered. And whatever we had been as a family stopped existing right there. With quiet decisions that kept choosing the wrong person over everyone else. Not long after that, Micky was diagnosed with breast cancer. When I first heard, I didn't believe it. I thought it was a joke. Or a misunderstanding. When I was younger, I didn't understand cancer. I thought breast cancer was something simple. Something you caught early. Something you went to the doctor for and then it was just gone. That's what I thought it was. I was living in Medford, working, trying not to feel anything. When she told me, I brushed it off. "It's nothing," I said. I had no idea. For the next two years, everything revolved around doctors. Referrals. Appointments. Scans. Specialists. They told her exactly what needed to be done. Surgery. A lymph node removal. A chance to stop it before it spread. They said it would help her. She didn't do it. Gideon convinced her she didn't need surgery. He told her God would heal her. That prayer was enough. That faith was stronger than medicine. That doctors didn't understand what God could do. So instead of surgery, they bought supplements. Instead of treatment, they bought a juicer. Every day, he made her juice. Green juice. Root juice. Things that promised miracles on the label and delivered nothing. He told her this was healing. That surgery was fear. That faith meant refusing it. She believed him.

Her cancer didn't stop. It grew. Quietly at first. Then faster. Then visibly. By the time she finally agreed to surgery, two years had passed. Two years too late. The damage was already done. Gideon had convinced her that God would save her. And she trusted him. Trusted prayer over medicine. Faith over reality. That was when something inside me broke. Not just trust. Faith. I watched someone I loved choose belief over survival. I watched religion turn into a weapon. I watched prayer replace action until there was nothing left to act on. That was when I lost my faith in God.

No one knew what was going to happen to Kasey and Karl. No one knew who would take them. No one knew where they would go. No one said it out loud, but everyone felt it hanging in the air. Micky didn't have much time left. Her body was disappearing in front of us. Weight falling off until there was almost nothing left to lose. By the end, she was barely eighty-eight pounds. She couldn't stand. She couldn't walk. Some days she couldn't even lift her head. So I left Medford. I went back to the house one more time. I moved in while she was dying.

I despised Gideon. Everything about him felt wrong. The way he spoke. The way he moved. The way he took up space without ever really being present. He talked like Kip from Napoleon Dynamite. Soft, awkward, detached from reality. A voice that never matched the weight of what he was doing to my family. I couldn't stand being in the same room as him. But it was her house. And it was her time. So I swallowed it, I buried it. There had been a plan. Mitchell was supposed to move out there. Take over the house. Raise Kasey and Karl. Pay the mortgage. Protect what was left. He hired a trust attorney. Put everything into a trust. Made sure it was legal. Clean. Proper. He always did things the right way. Then at the last minute, he couldn't do it. He couldn't leave his family in Los Angeles. And suddenly, there was no plan anymore. There was no one else. No backup. No safety net. So I stepped forward. I said I would do it. I was twenty-four years old. I had no idea what I was agreeing to. I just knew Kasey and Karl were innocent. I just knew they had already lost too much. I just knew I loved them. That was all the thinking I did. Micky kept getting smaller. Toward the end, every time she turned over in bed, you could hear it. A sharp crack. Another rib breaking. The last day she was alive was the Fourth of July. She couldn't walk. I lifted her out of bed and carried her outside in my arms. She felt lighter than she should have. Like holding someone who was already halfway gone. The backyard was full of noise. The last pieces of family we had left were there. Talking. Laughing. Pretending. Fireworks popping in the distance. Music drifting in from somewhere. Summer doing what summer does. Kasey ran through the sprinklers, giggling and laughing, water catching the light. Karl lit fireworks, eyes wide, proud of himself, alive in a way that hurt to look at. Everyone was smiling.

Micky sat in the chair, wrapped in blankets, staring out at it all with a distant look in her eyes. Not sad. Not scared. Just knowing.

Like she was already watching it from somewhere else. That day ruined the Fourth of July for me forever. Because every year after that, no matter where I am, I am back there. That porch. That light. That sound. That feeling that time was slipping through my fingers, and I couldn't stop it.

When it got late, I carried her back inside. Laid her back in bed. She didn't say much. She didn't need to. The next morning, I walked into her room and knew something was wrong before I reached the bed. She was gasping for air. Her eyes were wide. Confused. Searching my face like she was trying to remember where she was. She reached for my hand and grabbed it with what little strength she had left.

"I love," she said. "I love..." She tried again.

Her voice was barely there. "I love," and she said my name. Then her grip loosened.

I felt her hand go limp in mine. And then it slipped away completely. Just like that.

She was gone. Another parent gone.

I stood there holding nothing. And suddenly her life was mine. Her children. Her house. Her mortgage. Her unfinished story.

I was twenty-four years old. Already exhausted. Already carrying more than I knew how to name. Kasey and Karl were still there. Still breathing. Still looking to me. Thirteen and nine years old. So I stayed standing. And whatever came next, I was not prepared for it. Mitchell came down after she passed. The funeral was held at the church. Simple and Heavy in the way only real grief is. Everyone who was left showed up. There weren't many of us anymore. Afterward, we drove out to the cemetery in Selma. By the lake. The water was still. The kind of still that makes sound feel wrong. They buried her next to Kevin so they could be together forever. Side by side. Finally resting in the same place after all the chaos. I watched the dirt fall. I didn't cry. I felt empty. When it was over, we went back to the house. Gideon was still there. The house was quiet except for the garage. I saw him out there, moving slowly, pretending to stay busy. Touching tools that weren't his. Avoiding eye contact. Waiting to see what I would do. I walked toward him without rushing. He saw me coming. His shoulders stiffened. His hands stopped moving. He turned halfway, not fully. Like a cornered animal hoping stillness might save him. He already knew what was coming. Micky wasn't there anymore. There was no one left to shield him. No one left to choose him. I stepped close. Close enough that he had to look up at me. I didn't raise my voice. "Your time is up," I said. "Get the fuck out." He swallowed. His mouth opened. Nothing came out. He nodded once. Then he turned and started walking down the driveway. I followed him. Not fast. Not angry. Just there. Every few steps, I kicked a rock at his heels. Not hard. Not playful. Enough to keep him moving. Enough to let him feel it. I shoved his shoulder once. Then, at the end of the driveway, I slapped him across the back of his head. I hoped he would do something, so I could hurt him like he hurt my family. "Keep going," I said.

His voice came out thin. Weak. Almost breaking. "Okay." He didn't turn around again. By the time we reached the end of the driveway, his head was down. His face red. Tears sitting in his eyes, not falling. Humiliated in a way you can't fake or undo. He stepped onto the road. He turned around once last time, and I spat in his face as hard as I could. He did nothing. I watched him walk away. And that was it. I never saw him again. The house was quiet when I went back inside. For the first time in a long time, it felt like it belonged to us again. After that, everything became paperwork. Not grief. Not memories. Courts. Forms. Meetings. Signatures. Words like 'guardianship' and 'responsibility' felt too big to belong to me. I had to make it official. I had to become something I had never planned to be. I had to take care of Karl and Kasey. I didn't do it alone. Mitchell handled what I couldn't. He knew the system. He knew the language. He hired the right people. He paid for things I didn't even know how to ask for. Lawyers. Filings. Fees. Deadlines that would have crushed me if I had tried to face them by myself. Mitchell had money. But more than that, he had steadiness. He cared. He always called us his Godkids. All three of us. He said it casually, like it was obvious. Like it was a role he had already accepted long before anyone else noticed it was needed. At the time, I didn't always appreciate him. Sometimes I resented him.

He questioned me. Checked on me. Stepped in when I didn't want help. Sometimes it felt like he was trying to parent me, and I pushed against it the way young men do when they think they're already carrying enough. But looking back now, I see it clearly. I could not have done it without him. Not emotionally. Not financially. Not legally. Not at all. He held things together while I learned how to stand inside a life I never asked for. He made sure the house didn't disappear. That the kids didn't disappear. That everything didn't collapse all at once. When everything was finally set up, when the paperwork was signed, and the future was as stable as it could be, Mitchell went back to Los Angeles.

He left quietly. Like he always did. And I stayed. I was twenty-four years old. With two kids. A mortgage. A house full of ghosts. And a responsibility that didn't care how tired I was. That was the start of a new decade. A new life. A role I wasn't ready to volunteer for.

IO

ANGELS COME IN BLONDE

So, I WAS FINALLY on my own, and I quickly learned that owning a house was not for the weak. Everything would break constantly. Pipes would burst and freeze overnight, and I'd have to climb under the house and dig them out and figure out how to fix them. The well pump would go out, and I would have to fix the water pump to get water, drinking water. With no skill or knowledge in any of it. It was just one big ordeal after another, constantly. And I could never make ends meet. I got a little help. I received some money that covered the mortgage, the power, and some food from Kevin's survivor benefits when I became the children's guardian.

I used it to pay for the house and stuff, but that was it. Everything else, I had to come up with on my own and fix for years. It wasn't easy for me. And then parenting. I was never a parent before. I had no idea what I was doing.

I quickly became Micky because that's all I knew. I treated the kids like how she treated me, like verbatim, because that's all I knew. I never beat them or anything, because I wouldn't do that. I became very strict and had strict rules. After having kids of my own, I would have done it all differently. My goal the whole time was just to keep the house going, to just give my siblings a home. I found an envelope with my name on it in her safe. Inside was a voice recording of Micky. She talked to me for eleven straight hours. Footage she recorded in her bed the whole last year she was alive. She showered me with the sweetest things I've ever heard in my life. She'd say, "I never knew what real love was until you were born, and when you looked up at me and smiled, you were the first person who ever really loved me." She would say things like, "I want you to take care of those kids, and I want you to be smart with your money and give them good food. I just don't want them to not have a place to go. I want them to have a home, somewhere to belong." She just kept going hour after hour. Giving me advice about money, about the kids, about what to do, what not to do, in great detail. She filmed her voice like this into this recorder so I could always know how much she loved me. I heard it in her voice, and I still do to this day. In reality, I didn't even know what to do. I was so poor I couldn't even afford to buy them anything. No name-brand shampoo, generic from the dollar store. It was like that with everything. I did the best I could do. Even then, I felt like a failure. I wanted to give them more, but I just couldn't. Drowning by myself, I didn't know what to do. Then in walked Tayla into my life. She was the rock that held me together for the next four years. My first real long-time girlfriend. I had a thing for Tayla for years. She wouldn't give me the time of day. I noticed her long before she ever noticed me. And when everything fell apart. When Micky died. When the house became mine. The weight of adulthood landed all at once. Two weeks later, after it all fell down, Tayla finally agreed to go out with me.

Two weeks. I was still barely standing.

I was painfully shy. So shy, I barely spoke.

We went to the movies, and I don't think I said a single word the entire time. When she came over later and we hooked up, it was awkward. I was awkward. I didn't know how to exist inside my own body yet. But that part didn't last. We became inseparable almost immediately. One night turned into a few. A few nights turned into every night. And then suddenly, she was just there. Living there. Staying. Tayla grounded me.

She was tall, about five-eleven.

Long blonde hair. An angelic face that seemed to glow even in bad lighting.

She had a presence. The kind that made the world look at her. When we went places together, people stared. Guys stared. Women stared. She was beautiful in a way that didn't ask for attention but pulled it anyway. And I felt lucky. Really lucky. She didn't mother me. But she made sure things didn't fall apart. She was the angel on my shoulder when chaos tried to take over. She kept the lights on. She kept me pointed forward. I don't know if I could have done it without her. But there was something else with me too. A quieter voice. A darker one. It started after the football accident. The neck injury. Pills for pain from my doctor. Then pills for everything else. The grief. The pressure. The responsibility.

The noise in my head. The tension screaming in my neck. I kept taking more.

And more. And more. I still functioned.

I still showed up. I still took care of what I was supposed to take care of. For a long time, it worked. That's how addiction gets you. Slowly. Quietly. In the dark. It took years. But that was the beginning. The beginning of a long stretch of addiction.

When Tayla moved in, Dusty was still around. He had a kid by then. A girlfriend he lived with. They fought constantly. Loud, ugly fights. And every time it blew up, she would kick him out. No warning. No mercy. He would show up at my place and sleep on the couch. That couch.

Which is kind of ironic, looking back, considering where he would eventually end up. More successful than all of us. More than anyone would have ever guessed, while he was sleeping

there with nothing. She would kick him out with nothing. No toothbrush. No shampoo. No conditioner. Nothing.

And every time, he would ask me to buy him the basics, and I always did. Of course I did. Tayla used to joke that Dusty was my son. It was funny at first.

Then it wasn't. Somewhere along the way, Dusty started sliding into addiction too. Pills at first. Same as me. Then other things. I don't even know exactly when it crossed the line. I just know that it did.

I remember seeing him one day at the gym. The same gym where I first met him when we were young. But he didn't look like that Dusty anymore. He looked smaller. Hollowed out. Pale. Pale like a ghost. I didn't know exactly what he was doing. But I knew it wasn't good. We were brothers in addiction. Both of us stuck. Both of us aware. Talking about it sometimes, but completely unable to pull each other out. Two people drowning side by side, pretending we were still swimming. After Tayla moved in, strange things started happening. Real things.

She woke one night to find a figure standing over her. Not a shadow. A person. Standing there, watching her.

One night, my bedroom door got kicked in. Not opened. Kicked. Ten five-gallon water jugs flew into the room like someone had hurled them through the door with force. There was no explanation. No one there. One roommate said she saw a dark woman running through the garage. Not a person. Something else. She said it growled at her. Another roommate said she saw a woman in white dancing in our living room. Not standing. Dancing.

There were more things. Sounds. Shapes. Feelings. The kind you can't explain without sounding insane, but you know what you saw. You know what you felt. Karl would start screaming, blood-curdling screams at 3 am every night. Paralyzed by his sleep. Kasey would hear knocking on his window, and someone would say to come out and play through the window at 3 am. The house didn't feel empty. It felt occupied. So I called a priest. They came over and saged the house. Room by room. Smoke filling the air. Words spoken softly but firmly. Like they were pushing something out. After that, nothing ever happened again. Not one thing. The house went quiet. But the addiction didn't. If anything, it got worse. And that was when I knew whatever was haunting the house wasn't the scariest thing living there. As the years went by, we stayed together. But the pills didn't loosen their grip. They tightened it. About three years in, it stopped being manageable. It stopped being quiet. I would get sick without them. Real sick.

Withdrawals that crawled through my body. Panic attacks that came out of nowhere when I didn't have any left.

We called everyone we knew.

Anyone who might have pain pills.

Anyone who might know someone who did. I sold things to get them.

Anything that could turn into money.

It was getting out of control, and I knew it.

Tayla almost left me. More than once.

And every time, she would have been right to. Then something changed.

Not all at once. But enough to stop everything else in its tracks. A little while later, Tayla became pregnant. I remember the moment we found out for sure. We were sitting in a women's health clinic, staring at an ultrasound screen.

I was only expecting one. The tech paused. Tilted her head. Then smiled.

She said, "Oh, look. There's another one back there." I looked her dead in the eyes and told her to shut the fuck up and look again. I was young. Twenty-six. Maybe twenty-seven. Terrified and in denial all at once. She looked again. Then nodded.

Yep. Two. Two babies. Two lives. Two tiny heartbeats flickering on a screen. That was the moment I decided to stop the pills. Nine months later, I remember it as if it were yesterday. The hospital room. The bright lights. Tayla is going in for a C-section. And then they brought them out.

Two perfect baby boys. Healthy. Real.

Mine. Tayla was asleep, recovering.

And I was sitting there holding them.

One of them started crying. So I sang to him. You are my sunshine. My only sunshine. I held that tiny six-pound baby in my arms. Maybe seven pounds. And I sang until he calmed down. That was when I finally understood what Micky meant. That was real love. For the first time in my life. Everything before that moment stopped mattering. It just did. It felt good to matter to someone. To be needed. To see a piece of yourself living outside your own body. That was the day life actually began for me. Nothing before it mattered.

After the twins were born, everything got harder. I had never dealt with newborns before. Not really. Tayla had. She was incredible at it. She had this double-sided breastfeeding pillow, one baby on each side, and she handled it like it was second nature. Calm. Focused. Capable.

I was working early mornings. Six a.m. starts. Eventually, we started sleeping in separate rooms. Not because of some big decision. Just because that's what made it easier to survive the nights. Somewhere along the way, we faded. There was no explosion. No betrayal. No dramatic moment. After four or five years together, we didn't feel like partners anymore. We felt like friends. Like roommates. Like two people managing a life instead of living one. Then one day, we fought. I don't even remember what it was about now. I just remember saying it. Telling her to leave. Saying, "Fine. Just leave then."

I didn't think she would. But she did.

I was at work, or somewhere away from the house, when she rented a U-Haul. In the middle of nowhere. In that tiny town. She packed up her life. Years of it. Quietly. She hated living out there. She didn't drive. The house was isolated, miles from anything. She only left once a month. To see family. To grocery shop. That was it. She was trapped out there. With me. Looking back now, I think it was probably good that she left. She got to be free. She got to start her life instead of being stuck in the middle of nowhere, the way I was. She packed up, and she was gone. At first, I felt relief. Freedom.

I told myself I could hook up with anyone I wanted. Party. Do whatever I wanted. I felt light. Untethered. Like something had been lifted. That feeling didn't last.

Not even close. Then it hit me.

The 2015 breakdown. I had never experienced anything like it before. Not even when my parents died. This was

different. This was deeper. This was everything collapsing inward at once.

It was one of the hardest things I've ever lived through. And that's where this story really turns. I felt okay. Until I didn't.

The year before, I had quit smoking cigarettes and switched to vaping. When Tayla left, the vaping got out of control. I don't even know exactly why. Nerves. Being alone. The house being too quiet. The babies not being there all the time.

I still saw them constantly. I drove to where she moved and spent time with them. But it wasn't the same. I would come back to that house afterward, and suddenly I was alone in it. My siblings were technically there, but they were teenagers by then. School. Sports. Friends. Lives of their own. They were never really home. And when they were, they weren't there. I was. By myself. That's when the anxiety started.

Not normal anxiety. Not nerves. Something else. I was vaping every second of the day. Constantly. I would wake up in the middle of the night and vape. I couldn't stop. It did something to me mentally. Something snapped loose. I couldn't sleep. For two weeks straight, I did not sleep. Not real sleep. Not even close. I felt insane. My body

was exhausted, but my mind would not shut off. I couldn't sit still. I couldn't watch a movie. I couldn't focus on anything.

The only thing that helped was pacing.

I would walk around the property for hours. Around the porch. Back and forth. Over and over again. Trying to make it stop. It never stopped. I went to the ER multiple times. They gave me anxiety meds. Benzos. None of it helped. Not even a little. It didn't slow anything down. At one point, they gave me something called hydroxyzine. I took it, and for the first time in weeks, I actually fell asleep.

I slept for about three hours. When I woke up, it was the worst reaction I have ever had in my life. My skin felt like it was on fire. My entire body was burning. Not hot. Burning. I ripped my shirt off and started running around the house. I couldn't stop moving. It felt like my skin was on fire from the inside out. I was panicking. Completely out of control. I couldn't calm down. I couldn't make it stop.

I had to call an ambulance. They came, gave me something, and whatever they gave me finally stopped it. Just like that.

I went back to the ER again. I went to the ER seven times in about two weeks.

Finally, I went to my primary care doctor. I was in full crisis. I couldn't sit. I couldn't stop talking. I couldn't sleep. I couldn't exist inside my own head. They brought in a psychiatrist. She told me I was in crisis. She was right. I had lost my parents. I had lost my family home. And now I had lost the family I built.

Something broke. They started putting me on medication. Antidepressants. Antipsychotics. One of them was

Seroquel. Taking Seroquel was one of the worst experiences of my life.

I would fall asleep and have these violent, terrifying dreams. Like being on a roller coaster and suddenly flying off, falling through the air, crashing into the ground over and over again. The antidepressants were worse. I had never felt suicidal in my life. Not once. But on those meds, it was like a voice appeared. Quiet. Persistent. Telling me it was okay to end it. Telling me to kill myself. When that happened, I had to picture the twins. Their little baby faces. That was it. I would just keep seeing their faces over and over in my head. That was the only thing that

kept me there. The only thing that stopped me from listening to the voices. Just the image of them. That wasn't me.

That was the medication. Everything they gave me made it worse. Every single thing. More anxiety. More fear. More

disconnection. Nothing helped. Then, finally, I stopped vaping. I went back to smoking cigarettes. And almost immediately, everything stopped.

The anxiety vanished. I could sleep again. I felt normal. Like someone flipped a switch back on. After that, Tayla and I crossed paths a few times. We hooked up here and there. We talked. We spent time together. Once on her birthday, sex here and there, never constant. Moments that felt familiar but fragile. But after I finally processed losing her and losing the life we had built, we never got back

together. We tried a couple of times. It didn't work. About nine months to a year later, she met someone else. She's still with him to this day. That's where our story ended. We co-parent. Sometimes we're friends, sometimes not, sometimes we get along, sometimes we don't. I could have done worse, but I didn't with her.

That's where Tayla leaves this story.

II

FUCKBOYS

By 2016, I was single again. Stable. Clear. Back in my body. The breakdown was behind me. I was sleeping. Eating. Training. I lived in the gym. Lifting heavy. Running hard. I was in the best shape of my life, the kind of shape that comes from obsession, not vanity. I'd never really described myself before, but I stood out whether I wanted to or not. I'm six-foot-two. Black hair. Sharp features. The kind of face people study for a second longer than they mean to. My body was covered in tattoos. Not scattered ones. Not impulsive ones. Full sleeves. Hands. Chest. Back. Color everywhere. Work done by masters. Real art. Thirty thousand dollars worth of ink that looked less like decoration and more like a new skin. No two pieces matched anyone else's. Nothing generic. Nothing copied. Every tattoo was intentional, bold, and loud without begging for attention. When I walked into a room, people noticed. Not because I tried to be seen, but because there wasn't anyone else who looked like me. Anywhere. Women stared openly. Not subtle glances. Full eye contact. Smiles, they didn't bother hiding. Conversations started without effort. I didn't have to sell myself. I didn't have to explain anything. Attraction happened before words.

It wasn't arrogance. It was physics.

I was the kind of guy people whispered about after I passed. The kind you don't see twice in the same place. The kind that doesn't blend in, no matter how quiet he tries to be. On paper, I was everything you're supposed to want. Healthy. Stable. Driven. Dangerous-looking but controlled. The outside finally matched the intensity I'd always carried inside. And for the first time in a long time, I felt powerful again.

Around that time, Jameson called me from Los Angeles. He sounded tired. Older. Slower in a way I hadn't heard before. He told me he wanted me to come down with a U-Haul and take his things. All of them. He had money.

Collections. Antiques. Objects that carried weight and history. A life's worth of proof. He said he wanted me to have it. Said he didn't trust his ex-wife or her son. Said he felt like if I didn't come, it would all disappear. I was young. Distracted. Buried in responsibility. The house. The kids. Everything pulling at me at once. I told him not to worry about it. Said it was fine. Said I couldn't make the drive. I would regret that later. Deeply. But that part comes after. Not long after that, Dusty moved to Minnesota. Just like that, he was gone. Far enough away that seeing him again felt theoretical. We'd lived entire lives together, and now the distance was measured in states and seasons. But we didn't disappear from each other. We moved online. Dusty and I had always drawn people in. Not on purpose. Not strategically. It just happened. Wherever we went, people watched. On Facebook, especially. We had voices that people recognized. Opinions people reacted to. Energy that didn't sit quietly. It started simple. Comment threads. Public jokes. Teasing each other. Talking shit back and forth in a way that felt sharp but playful. Honest but funny. Nothing rehearsed. People started showing up just to watch. They didn't care what we were talking about. They cared about how we talked. What we'd say next. Who would go harder? Who would cross the line first?

There was a rhythm to it. A chemistry. We understood each other's timing instinctively. When to push. When to pull back. When to let something hang.

It wasn't cruelty. It was banter with teeth. From Minnesota to Oregon, we kept it going. Posts. Comments. Callouts. Threads that grew faster than we expected. Notifications stacking. Names we didn't recognize chiming in like they'd been there the whole time. People weren't just reading. They were waiting. I remember the moment it clicked. I messaged Dusty and suggested we start a group. Not about anything specific.

Not a cause. Not a movement. Just us. The same back and forth. The same voices that everyone wanted to hear. That's how Fuckboys was born.

At the beginning, none of us even knew what the hell we were building. It wasn't a plan. It wasn't a brand. It wasn't a vision. It was just a group. A dumb idea that kept growing because we kept feeding it. We added people manually, over and over, like we were shoveling coal into a furnace we didn't understand. People would get pissed, remove themselves, talk shit about it, and then we'd just add them right back in. Again. And again. They hated that we wouldn't let them leave. That only made it louder. At first, it was just me and Dusty talking shit. Endless back and forth. Inside jokes. No structure. No rules. Just noise. And when we hit two hundred members, I remember stopping and thinking, holy shit, there are two hundred people watching us do this. Reading it. Reacting to it. We laughed like it was nothing. Like it wasn't already something. That was around the same time Dusty left the group entirely. On to different things. The machine kept moving with me at the helm. Within the same beat, Randy entered. He had been around for years, just a side character, finally stepping into the spotlight. When Dusty left, he filled a huge empty space; new management, same goal. Randy was my right-hand man, my ride or die, and he still is to this day. I had brothers, but he was like the brother I always wanted. If I were the President of the Group, Randy would be the VP.

Dusty decided to step away to chase modeling, Instagram, his own thing. He didn't disappear from my life, but he disappeared from the group. And suddenly, it was just me. No balance. No counterweight. No one to pull me back when I went too far. So I leaned into it. Somewhere around that moment, I created a character.

Not consciously at first. It just happened. A version of me that wasn't me. Louder. Crueler. Untouchable. Cocky in a way that made people furious. Chad-like. The kind of guy you hated on sight but couldn't stop watching. The kind of guy who said exactly what you weren't supposed to say and

enjoyed the silence afterward. I had no filter.

I talked shit to everyone. It didn't matter who they were. Didn't matter how big they thought they were. If someone came at me, I didn't defend myself. I humiliated them. If they pushed again, I banned them.

Gone. No debate. No explanation.

Inside the group, I created a false reality.

I was the authority because I said I was. If anyone questioned it, they were erased. And the thing is, people hated that too. But their friends were in the group. Everyone in town talked about it. Screenshots spread. Stories traveled. Even the people who despised me stayed because leaving meant being outside the conversation. As the months and years went on, the numbers kept climbing. One thousand. Two thousand. Five thousand. Ten thousand. Twenty thousand. Every milestone felt unreal for about ten seconds. Then it was on to the next one. And somewhere in that climb, something shifted. I didn't notice it all at once. It showed up in fragments. Whispers when I walked by. People knowing my name when I didn't know theirs. Being recognized in places I'd always been invisible before. Girls leaning toward each other and saying, that's him. That's him.

Before this, I was just another guy at a bar. Maybe I'd hook up here and there. Maybe I'd get lucky at a bar or party. Nothing special. Nothing consistent. Now it was different. Girls wanted to talk to me because they knew me. They wanted to sleep with me because I was known. Not because of who I was, but because of what I represented. And I didn't understand that yet. I just felt the power of it. Fame, even small fame, does something dangerous.

It compresses reality. It makes the world feel smaller, and you feel bigger inside it. Everywhere you go, people react. They laugh before you speak. They watch your mouth like it might detonate. You stop being a person and start being a moment.

And I loved it. As the group grew, so did the character. The persona stopped being something I turned on and off. It

followed me into real life. The arrogance. The disregard. The sense that consequences were optional. I started believing the version of myself I had invented for entertainment. By the time we hit numbers that didn't make sense anymore, I was gone inside it. Fifty thousand. One hundred thousand. Then numbers so large they stopped feeling real.

And then one day, we hit one million.

One million people. I remember staring at the number as if it were a typo. Like someone had added an extra zero by mistake.

But it stayed. And from that point on, there was no escaping it. I'd travel through Oregon. Portland. Eugene. Corvallis. Small towns. Big cities. It didn't matter. I'd walk into a bar, and people already knew me. Girls would come up to me as we'd met before. Like I owed them something. Like they already had a version of me in their head. Everyone knew who I was. I knew almost none of them. That's when it stopped being fun and started being something else. That's when the character fully replaced the person. I had become the thing I created. And the worst part was, everyone loved him.

Except me. By then, I felt untouchable.

People I banned didn't just disappear. They splintered off. They started their own versions of the group. Cheap reflections. Off-brand rebellions. They gave themselves names like the "Heathens", "The Misfits", "The Fuck Daddys."

Slapped decals on their cars, tried to recreate the energy they'd been kicked out of. But they couldn't. They were imitations. I wasn't fast food. I wasn't even a chain. I was the source. They were knockoffs trying to sell the same product without the poison that made it addictive. Amazon versus Wish. Everyone could tell the difference. And the original had grown into something I no longer controlled.

The group was too big. Thousands of posts a day. Chaos moving faster than any single person could manage. I had to bring in moderators. Admins. People just keep the machine running. It wasn't a community anymore. It was an ecosystem. It fed on attention, conflict, validation, and humiliation. I would make posts, best boob challenge. Best booty challenge. Let me rate you. Hundreds of women would post, begging me to notice them, begging me to validate them. I felt like Jameson was in Hollywood, but more powerful. I felt like a God, and they treated me like one.

That was the power of it. Not attraction. Control. The knockoff groups tried to copy that, too. They never could. They didn't have the gravity. They didn't have me. I remember one night at a grocery store. Parking lot half full. A cluster of cars off to the side. Fifteen people, maybe more, all part of one of the imitation groups. They recognized me immediately. Whispering. Then louder. Talking shit. Posturing in a group like that meant something. I just looked at them. Slowly nodded. A silent challenge. Do something. None of them did.

I got in my car and left. That's how real it felt. Not just online. In the real world.

The persona didn't shut off when I logged out.

People reacted to me the same way everywhere. Fear. Hate. Admiration. Curiosity. All of it tangled together. The group wasn't just digital anymore. People met through it. Organized through it. They planned trips. Parties. Entire weekends. There was a camping event that turned into a small city. Hundreds of cars. Tents as far as you could see. Music. Noise. Chaos.

And when I showed up, it went quiet in a way that still makes my skin crawl.

They treated me like a god. They called me "King Fuckboy." Half joke. Half belief. People lined up just to be near me. To be seen near me. A core group formed around it all. The most loyal. The loudest. The ones who defended me no matter what. They called themselves the Fucks. They lived for it. The group was their identity. We had characters, the characters' plot, and the moderators and admins became like celebrities with their own reality tv show and I was the center of it. Every controversy. Every argument. Every surge of attention ran through me. This one girl and her friend slept with me at the same time so that I would make her admin for a day, and I found it hilarious. If I ever left the group, it collapsed. I tested that more than once. This went on for years; I'd step away. The energy would drain out of it. Moderators tried to keep it alive. Tried to imitate the tone. Tried to become me. It never worked.

When I came back, it roared back to life. Louder than before. Hungrier. Like it had been holding its breath. That cycle repeated. Leave. Return. Explode. Each time feeding the myth that I was the only thing keeping it alive. And I started to believe it too. The reach of it was insane. Relationships formed because of that group. Marriages. Divorces. Countless children were born. Entire lives rerouted because two people met inside something I created while talking shit. That's the part people don't understand about influence.

It isn't just followers. It's consequences. Ripples you never see. Babies born.

Families started. Families broken. All traced back to a place that started as a joke.

And the worst part is, while all of that was happening, I didn't feel powerful because of what I built. I felt powerful because of what it gave me. And that feeling is the most dangerous drug there is. One November night, it was my thirtieth birthday party. I remember walking up to the house and already knowing something was wrong in the best way. The lights were on in every room. Cars lined the street like a concert had just let out. Music leaked through the walls before I even touched the door. When it opened, it was chaos already in motion. People everywhere, shoulder to shoulder, red cups in hands, laughter ricocheting off the ceiling. Someone yelled my name and suddenly the room shifted toward me like a tide. This wasn't a party starting. It was a party waiting.

Girls I recognized. Girls I didn't. Faces from old nights, old stories, half-remembered mornings. People who had driven hours. People who shouldn't all know each other but somehow did. Nine hundred bodies in a house that could barely breathe. Heat. Sweat. Noise. Every conversation overlaps, every glance lands on me for just a second too long. Then the music changed. The opening beat of Pony by Ginuwine hit and the room snapped. Hands grabbed me. Laughing, shouting, pulling me forward. Someone slapped the pool table and the crowd opened up around it like a circle in a fight scene. They told me to get up there. Chanting. Phones already out. I climbed onto the felt, the lights blurring, the bass thumping through my ribs. For a moment there was silence. Then I moved. Not carefully. Not shy. I danced like I belonged there. Like this was what they had come to see. The room exploded. Money came first. Bills fluttering through the air, landing on the table, sticking to my skin. Then the quarters. Sharp little impacts. Metallic clinks. I could feel them bouncing, spinning, rolling off the edge. I stripped without thinking. Shirt gone. Shoes kicked away. The crowd roared louder every time something hit the floor. I straddled the table, hands on the felt, hips moving with the beat, eyes locked with people I barely knew who were screaming like they did. I took everything off until there was nothing left. For those minutes, nothing else existed. Not tomorrow. Not consequences. Not the quiet that comes later. I was the center of the room. The gravity. Every camera pointed at me. Every voice feeding the moment. It felt like fame, even if it wasn't. It felt like being chosen. Like I mattered enough for the world to stop and watch. That night, I wasn't just at my birthday party. I was the show online and off. That wasn't the only time I took my clothes off for money. One night, I went downtown to the local strip club. It was amateur night, where a local celebrity such as myself could get up on that stage and shine. The place was already shaking before we even got inside. People squeezed into a place that should have held half the people waiting outside. Bass rattling the windows. Neon bleeding through the dark. Bodies pressed together like a riot that forgot why it started. Amateur night. Guy's night. The kind of night where the rules bend because the room decides they do. We walked in as a unit. Twelve hundred people crammed into a space meant for maybe three hundred. Sweat in the air. Cheap liquor. Smoke machines coughing haze across the ceiling. The stage lights flicked on and off like a warning. You could feel the crowd before you saw it. Loud. Hungry. Ready for something to happen. They announced the sign-up. We didn't hesitate. Me and a few guys from the crew climbed onto the stage edge, scribbled our names down, grinning like we were about to jump off a roof. The crowd noticed immediately. Whispers spread. Heads turned. People pointing. There was already a charge around us, like the room recognized something before it understood it. The first guy went up. The noise was instant. Cheers rip through the club, drowning out the DJ. Money flying early. The second guy went up, and it got louder. Way louder than anyone else that night. The staff started looking confused. The DJ leaned forward. The bouncers smirked. Then my name was called. The room erupted like a bomb had gone off. Not polite applause. Not curiosity. Recognition. People screaming like I had just walked onstage at a show they paid to see. I stepped under the lights, and it hit all at once. Heat. Sound. Eyes. Hundreds of them. Phones up. Drinks sloshing. Bills already in the air. The opening riff of Rock You Like a Hurricane by the Scorpions tore through the speakers. I didn't rush it. I moved slow at first, letting the music build, letting the crowd lean in. Every beat landed heavier. Every cheer got louder. I stripped with confidence, not performance. Like I owned the space. Like I belonged there more than the stage itself. The crowd fed it back to me tenfold. I took everything off and let everything hang out as I danced. Money rained down. Not tossed. Thrown. Bills slapping the stage, sliding across the floor, sticking to sweat. I took off more than anyone else did that night and the place lost its mind every single time. People pounding tables. Staff yelling over each other. The DJ replaying the chorus because the crowd demanded it. For that 10 minutes, the club revolved around me. When the music finally cut and I stepped back, breathing hard, lights flickering, the stage looked like a battlefield made of cash. I glanced down and laughed. Over a thousand dollars scattered at my feet. But it wasn't about the money. It was the roar. That sound when a room that size decides you are the moment. When strangers chant your name like they know you. When the noise feels alive, like it could carry you somewhere dangerous if you let it. That night wasn't a stunt. It was a peak. The kind you remember forever because you know, even while it's happening, that it will never happen the same way again. After a while, I got sick of the constant sex revolving door of women, who I didn't even bother to learn their names. After a while I met a girl who stood above the rest. She looked unreal. Short. Perfect. Like something manufactured. A model's body in a Barbie-sized frame. The kind of woman who didn't just turn heads, she stopped conversations. In the group, she was untouchable. Thousands of guys watched her from a distance, waiting for a chance they were never going to get. And she chose me. Not because she knew me, but because of what I was. Because I was the king. The center. The gravity everything bent toward. We started seeing each other, and against my better judgment, I fell hard. Faster than I ever should have. Hard enough to ignore the cracks. She had a secret. A secret made out of fine little white powder. A cocaine problem she hid well. I didn't use. She knew that. So she lied. She said she was sick on the Fourth of July. Too sick to see me. That same night, another guy from the group posted pictures with her. Fireworks in the background. Smiles, she claimed, weren't real. She told me the photos were old. From another year. They weren't. She broke up with me shortly after. Clean. Quick. No closure. And it shattered something in me that was already unstable. That's when a new spiral started. I'd been reckless before. But after that, I became destructive. The options were endless. Messages poured in faster than I could open them. Dozens an hour. Women from different towns. Different cities. Everyone wanted to sleep with me. Everyone wanted me, so I gave myself to everyone. I moved through it like it didn't matter. One girl in one town, another in the next town, and one on the way home. Boom, boom, boom, night after night, for a long time. Not because I was enjoying it. Because I was running. I had more sex than most people will ever have in several lifetimes. I see the pattern now. I always do this. When I get hurt, I act out. I numb it with attention. With bodies a lot of them. With distraction. It looks like confidence from the outside. It's really avoidance. That phase lasted years. I wasn't famous in the way people think of fame. Not national. Not universal. But locally, regionally, I was known. Oregon knew me. The group had people everywhere, but the epicenter was there. Almost famous. Enough that my name meant something when I walked into a room. One night I sent my siblings to their friend's house. Then it all peaked. A party in the woods at Kevin and Micky's house in Selma. It was mine then, but I still felt them there. A house that should have held maybe twenty people. That night, it held thousands. Cars lined the road for over a mile down the street. Parked in ditches. Between trees. On shoulders that barely existed. All the way down the driveway on both sides. Music bled into the forest. Live bands, lights cut through the dark. People everywhere. Inside. Outside. On the roof. In fields. It was chaos in the purest form. Like Project X, but real. Louder. Dirtier. No cameras controlling it. No script. Just excess feeding itself. Alcohol. Noise. Movement. Sex and orgies everywhere, in the pool, in the hot tub, in every bedroom, bathroom, and closet. Even in the middle of the living room and outside against trees, for everyone to see. The kind of night that feels historic while it's happening and catastrophic the next morning. And at the center of it was me. People treated me like I built the place. Like I owned the night. Like I was the reason they were there. It felt godlike in the most dangerous way. Like I had created a world and invited people to live inside it. The night ended with sixteen cop cars coming to my house. Complete with two ambulances, a helicopter, and a fire truck. It was the wildest party Southern Oregon had ever seen. In the aftermath, you realize worlds like that don't last. They burn out. They collapse under their own weight. Fame always does. Attention turns. Energy fades. Eventually, even the noise gets exhausting. I got sick of it. So I left. Not all at once. Not cleanly. But eventually, I stepped away. The group kept going, but it was never the same. I carried that energy with me onto my own social media. Smaller scale. Different platforms. I would do my own social experiments. Like, one time, it started as a joke. Or at least that's what I told myself. I kept seeing women talk about how bad it was online. The messages. The entitlement. The stuff they just quietly absorb every day because there's no point explaining it to people who refuse to hear it. I didn't fully believe it. Not because I thought they were lying, but because the scale of it felt exaggerated. Unreal. Like one of those things you nod at without ever actually feeling. So I decided to feel it. I created a new identity. A twenty-two-year-old fitness influencer. Blonde. Smiling. Perfect lighting. I named her Rebekah Chambers. A friend handed over photos and enough content to make the illusion airtight. Gym shots. Mirror selfies. Captions with just enough vulnerability to seem human but not enough to scare anyone away. Then I hit post. Within minutes, the phone started buzzing. At first, it was flattering in a detached, sociological way. Compliments. Fire emojis. People asking about workouts. Then the tone shifted. Messages stacked on top of each other faster than I could read them. Over a hundred a day, then more, every day. Men asking where I lived. Men asking when we could meet. Men assuming that because I existed online, I was available offline. Some of them were strangers. Some of them were not. Guys I knew. Guys I had beers with, friends. Sliding into my inbox, like I was a real person on the other side of the screen. The messages got darker. Weirder. More desperate. Photos I never asked for. Requests that made me stare at the ceiling and laugh because the alternative was feeling sick. Offers to pay my phone bill. Offers to "take care of me." One guy picked up a second job just so he could send money to someone who did not exist. Paychecks. Rent. Groceries. Attention bought in installments. In thirty days, I made fifty-seven hundred dollars without ever meeting a single person. When I didn't respond fast enough, the mood flipped. Compliments turned to insults. Demands. Missed calls. Voice messages. Men spiraling because a stranger didn't validate them on schedule. A few offered ridiculous sums for me to fart in a jar, put my panties in, and send it to them. Sentences real people don't type loud. And the whole time, I just sat there. Watching. Taking notes. I wondered how women survive this without losing their minds. The craziest part was not the money or the messages. It was how normal it all felt to them. How entitled. How casual. Like this was just how the world worked and I was the weird one for questioning it. After thirty days, I shut it down. Deleted the account. Closed the inbox. Let Rebekah disappear. And I just stared at my phone, quiet for the first time in a month, thinking the same thing over and over. What the hell did I just do? What I learned was simple and horrifying. Guys can be disgusting. Attention is currency. Being hot is a cheat code. And the world treats you very differently when it thinks you are a girl. Funny experiment. Terrible reality. I went back to being myself with a new respect for women and a lingering sense that I had peeked behind a curtain I was never supposed to lift. I posted all as if this was a character of a reality show that everyone watched. They ate it up, they always did. The same presence as the group, the same gravity. And people followed. They still do. After being out of the group for a long time. Years later, I went back in one last time. Quietly, I deleted every comment I'd ever made. Every post. Every trace. Years of running that world, erased line by line. Then I left the group for good and blocked myself from it. No announcement. No goodbye. It was like I'd never existed there at all. And somehow, that was the most honest ending it could have had.

12

LEAVING HELL

RUNNING THAT HOUSE ALONE was never part of the plan. The mortgage didn't care about grief. The bills didn't care about responsibility. And the house was too big to carry quietly. Six bedrooms.

Four thousand square feet. 5 acres of land. Rooms that echoed even when no one spoke. So I did what felt practical. I rented it out. Craigslist ads. Short conversations. Cash deposits. No background checks. No real rules. If someone had the money, I let them move in. At the time, it felt like survival. Later, I understood it was desperation. The first guy was fine at first. Friendly. Normal. Paid on time. Then slowly, something shifted. He started taking space that wasn't his. Speaking like he owned the place. One day, he told me he was only paying half the rent now. Not asked. Told. When I tried to push back, his eyes changed. Flat. Cold. Like he was measuring me. The situation escalated fast. Threats without words. Tension that lived in every hallway. I slept lightly. I watched doors. I genuinely thought he might kill me. That was the first time I understood what it meant to lose control of your own house. After him came a couple.

They brought animals into the room. The smell spread everywhere. It soaked into the walls, the carpet, the air. They dropped acid in the living room like it was normal. Laughter at odd hours. Furniture rearranged without asking. My home stopped feeling like mine. Then there was the couple upstairs. The guy wasn't unstable in a dramatic way. He was worse than that. Calm. Reckless. Proud of it. He told me outright he was going to do drugs and didn't care what I thought. There was some kind of deal that went bad. I never got the full story. I just know it ended with this guy beaten up on my stairs. When I walked in from work. After that, I couldn't get him out. He refused to leave. Refused to negotiate.

Refused to care. Eventually, I paid him two hundred dollars just to disappear. Handed it to him and watched him walk out.

When the door closed behind him, I felt something release in my chest. Relief so strong it almost knocked me over. I stood there alone in the silence and realized how low I had sunk just to keep things from exploding. There was a girl who lived there for a while. It was fine until it wasn't.

We went out. She brought a friend. Bad decisions layered on top of exhaustion and alcohol. Lines crossed, a threesome happened. A problem that most men don't ever experience, but happened to me like clockwork weekly. After that, the dynamic collapsed. She moved out. Another room empty. Another reminder that nothing in that house stayed for long. And then there was Cody. The only one who didn't feel like a threat. The only one who didn't take more than he was given. But by then, the damage was already done. The house had become a revolving door of instability. Every new person brought a new risk. Every month felt like a gamble. I wasn't just paying a mortgage anymore. I was managing chaos.

I thought I was holding everything together.

In reality, I was barely keeping the walls from caving in. That house didn't just hold people. It absorbed them. And it was starting to absorb me too. My favorite of the bunch was Cody. He had his own damage. You could see it right away. The kind you don't learn in school. Prison stories. Gang-adjacent history. A life that had taught him how to survive before it taught him how to be soft. On the outside, he was rough. Sharp edges. Guard up. A presence that filled a room without trying to. But underneath that, he was like me. Just a person who came from nothing. Just a dad trying to do right by his kid. Just someone trying to stay alive long enough to matter. That's why it worked. At least for a while. We talked a lot. Late nights. Cigarettes outside. Conversations that drifted between bullshit and real without warning. We fought sometimes, sure, but it never felt dangerous. It felt human. Like two people who didn't know how to communicate without friction. There was one night I still laugh about, even now. Cody and Karl got into it. I don't even remember why. By then Karl was grown. Bigger than me. Strong. Not a kid anymore, pretty much an adult. I just remember chaos. Raised voices. Then suddenly Cody had Karl locked up, latched onto him like he wasn't letting go, no matter what. And then Karl's girlfriend, without hesitation, stuck her thumb straight up Cody's ass. Just like that. Cody froze. Let go immediately. Fight over. It was insane. Completely unhinged. The kind of moment that only happens in houses like that, in lives like ours. We stood there afterward, stunned, half laughing, half wondering how the hell we got there. That was Cody.

Unpredictable. Real. Ridiculous. He was a farmer too. The medical kind. We had acres out back, and he worked it. Made his money quietly. No flash. No bragging. Just work. But like everything in that house, nothing stayed stable forever. We argued sometimes. I don't even remember why. None of it feels important now. What I remember is that one day he was just... gone. A year of living together and then nothing. He left like a hurricane. Stuff everywhere. Messes I didn't recognize. Silence where there had been noise. I walked through the house afterward feeling that familiar emptiness again. Another person erased without ceremony.

The weirdest part? My TV remote disappeared. I searched everywhere. Weeks. Months. Gave up eventually. Years later, Cody and I reconnected.

Time had softened everything. The anger. The distance. The stories we told ourselves about each other. I went over to his place.

And there it was. My remote. Just sitting there like it had never left. We laughed about it. Hard. After everything, after all the chaos, after the fights, the exits, and the mess, we ended up good again. Real friends. The kind that survives distance, damage, and time. Some people don't stay in your life continuously. They leave. They come back. They circle. Cody was one of those. And somehow, through all of it, he stayed good. So did I.

Becoming a father didn't flip a switch for me. It didn't arrive like a clean ending or a redemption arc. It came in pieces. At first, I barely had them. One night a week. Sometimes two. Then three as they got older. I existed in this strange split reality where half my life was responsibility, and the other half refused to die. When I had the kids, everything slowed down. No parties. No

girls. No chaos. I stayed home. I cooked. I watched cartoons. I became quiet. Focused. Present.

Then, the moment they left, the other version of me woke back up.

For the first few years, I lived both lives at the same time. Father on rotation. Party kid the rest of the week. I told myself I could balance it. That I had control. And maybe for a while, I did.

Randy was always there when I didn't have my kids. The new era version of Dusty. Same energy. Same gravity toward trouble. Wherever he went, something happened. Wherever I followed, it got worse. Portland was one of those nights. A hotel room. Alcohol. Music too loud. A girl who recognized me from the page and wanted to see if the version online was real. Randy put the room on his card. The night blurred. In the morning, the sheets looked like a crime scene. Blood everywhere because she started her time of the month. It looked like a horror movie. Randy lost his mind, convinced he was about to be charged for everything. He wasn't. That part was funny. The rest was just chaos. Another time, a club. Two girls. Another hotel. Everyone drunk. Everyone reckless. They tried to turn it into a transaction and make us pay afterward. We laughed.

Told them no. They called some guy waiting outside in a van to scare us into paying. We didn't blink. We waited them out, slipped out the back, and checked out early. He never found us. We were already gone and we never paid! That was the pattern. Something intense. Something stupid. No consequences.

Repeat. I had a work Christmas party one year. Two nurses. My house. Doors closed. Lights low. Randy was too drunk to function, naked on the couch like he forgot where he was, after he slept with his girl. She came to my room. Crawled on all fours, like she was still hungry. She climbed up into my bed naked. And just started going down on my girl. They took turns going down on me, and then down on each other. I bent them both over my bed, stacked them on top of each other, and took turns with them. Screaming, orgasms, wet spots, a man who knew what he was doing. Afterward, they both just lay there, legs twitching. They couldn't move, they couldn't breathe. Placed in a sex coma, I knew my job there was done. I went out to see Randy snoring on my couch like a bear, naked and had no idea what had just happened. It wasn't just sex. It was dominance. Reaction. Control. I called an Uber for them, and they both limped out to the cab. I watched them leave with a smile. I was not one to ever be messed with. If someone ever came at me sideways, I made sure they regretted it. One of them started with a message that should have been ignored. A random name. A profile picture I didn't recognize. Paragraphs unloading all at once. She hated my posts. Hated my face. Hated my existence. Said I was attention seeking. Said I was a douchebag. Said I deserved to die alone. The kind of message that feels rehearsed, like she'd been waiting for a reason to send it. Most people would block her. I got even, so I clicked. Scrolled. Dug a little. Not deep. Just enough to find a place of work. A salon. Eugene. Two hours away. The idea hit me all at once, and I laughed out loud alone in my kitchen. I booked an appointment. A Brazilian. Under a fake name. For the next day. I posted about it, of course. Let the internet chew on it. The reactions came fast. People laughing. People horrified. People telling me I was insane. Someone commented, "You won't." That sealed it. The drive was long. Too long to back out without admitting defeat. Two hours to Eugene, Oregon, radio on. Coffee cooling in the cup holder. The joke was slowly mutating into something heavier the closer I got. By the time I pulled into the parking lot, it wasn't funny anymore. It was quiet. Clean. Normal. A place where nothing like this should happen. I walked in. She came out from the back, looked up, and froze. Not shock. Recognition. Her face went blank like she'd seen a ghost. No words. No apology. She turned around and walked straight back into the hallway. The air shifted. The front desk went silent. A manager stepped in fast, polite smile stretched thin, asking if someone else could take me. I said no. I told her I drove two and a half hours. I said I needed Karen. Minutes passed. Long ones. Then footsteps. Fast. Angry. She came back with eyes sharp enough to cut glass and motioned for me to follow her. No small talk. No professionalism left to hide behind. Just tension you could taste. The room was cold. I undressed completely. The silence was deafening. No music. No chatter. Just wax strips and breathing and the kind of quiet that feels deliberate. Every movement was clipped. Efficient. Furious. Each pull felt personal. Two strangers locked in a situation neither of us could escape without breaking the rules. When it was over, she stepped back. I stood up. Met her eyes. Calm. "I'm going to tell this story to our grandchildren one day." She looked like she might actually kill me. I got dressed slowly. Thanked no one. Walked out as if nothing happened. Sunlight hit my face. The door closed behind me. The world continued exactly as it always does after something insane. I drove home sore, exhausted, and laughing at the fact that this is how some chapters of life insist on being written. Not heroic. Not smart. Just unforgettable. It was petty. Cruel. Satisfying in the ugliest way. I was like that back then. I didn't let anything go. I made examples. I weaponized attention. I posted people to my following. I turned embarrassment into entertainment. I wasn't someone you wanted to challenge. Around that time, my grandmother, Jennifer, moved back from Hollywood. She had lived there through everything. The parties. The fame. The alcohol. All of it. When she came back, she wasn't glamorous anymore. Just bitter. Distant. A woman who had burned through every version of herself and didn't have much left for anyone else. She ended up in a nursing home. We weren't close. Then one day, they found her body hunched over her walker, dead. Gone. Just like that. No goodbye. No audience. The paper ran a small headline. Elizabeth Taylor double dies in Grants Pass. That was the summary of a whole life. All that beauty. All that attention. All that noise. Reduced to a few lines and a quiet room. She died alone. Looking back now, it all connects. The chaos. The control. The way I lived like nothing could touch me. The way fatherhood slowly pulled me away from it, piece by piece, until partying faded and being a dad took over completely. But in those early years, I was still both men. And one of them was dangerous. Another trip. Another city. Same rhythm. Always with Randy. He had this thing where he treated the world like a stage, and everyone on it was an extra. We would be walking down the street, and he would stop random strangers just to ask them if we went to high school together. Dead serious. Watching people panic, search their memory, and second-guess themselves. I would just stand there smiling, already knowing how it ended. We went to a Chinese restaurant, and he decided he was going to be blind for the entire meal. Sunglasses on. Head tilted back. Talking louder than necessary. When the bill came, he tried to hand the server his Food stamps card like it was a credit card. She stared at it, then at him, then at me. I lost it. We laughed the whole way out the door. That was how it always was. No plan. Just motion. We spent nights walking between bars, him too drunk to get in anywhere, me standing outside with him, making him chug water like a coach trying to sober up a fighter between rounds. We would wait. Try again. Sometimes it worked. Sometimes it didn't. Either way, we stayed out until something happened. Then Jamison called. He said he was on his way out, said he was dying. Said it quietly. Like he was telling me the weather. So we drove through the night. Twelve hours straight to LA. No sleep. Just headlights and silence. When we got there, I almost didn't recognize him. The man I remembered had filled rooms. Loud. Magnetic. Powerful. He knew everyone. Had everything. Money. Women. Influence. He was the kind of man you assumed would never weaken. But there he was. Lying in a nursing home bed. Skin and bone. Barely there. The body is still breathing, but the presence is already gone. I hugged him carefully. Sat with him. Looked at his face and tried to connect it to the man I had known. A couple of days later, he was dead. He was right about the money, about his possessions. His wife stole it all. What should have been generational wealth turned into scraps. Pennies. Another story for another time. After that, we went out in LA. And that was when it hit me. In Oregon, we were something. People knew us. Watched us. Reacted to us. Down there, we were nothing. No status. No recognition. Just two guys in a city that doesn't care unless you matter. I walked from club to club, trying to talk to women. None of them looked at me twice. One of them asked me for one hundred just to talk to her. That was the price. Attention had a number attached to it. Fame had a value. Without it, you were invisible. It was wild how fast the attraction disappeared when the status wasn't attached. How quickly confidence meant nothing if no one knew your name. That was just what we did back then. Trips. Chaos. Nights that blurred together. Running toward things without thinking about where they ended. And somewhere in the background of all of it, fatherhood kept pulling at me. Slowly. Quietly. Waiting for its turn. By then, my siblings were finally grown. On paper. They went off into the world and started their own lives. The trust said it was time. Time to sell the house. Time to close it out. Time to leave. I had been waiting for that moment longer than I could admit. I didn't want memories anymore. I wanted distance. I wanted a clean break from a place that had held too much. But the house didn't let go easily. I had roommates at the time. They seemed 100 percent normal when I let them move in, like church people, god people. I learned quickly that no one was ever who they pretended to be. They didn't respect the place. Didn't respect me. Drugs crept in secretly at first, then took over everything. Meth. Heroin. People I didn't know.

People I didn't trust. Tweakers who treated the house like a waypoint instead of a home. Cars started showing up at all hours. Not visitors. Not friends. Just vehicles idling too long. Parking where they shouldn't. Leaving. Coming back. Watching. Windows in the driveway getting smashed like warnings. Glass everywhere. The sound of it would echo through the trees and sit in my chest long after the noise stopped. The house was mostly empty by then. Nothing left in most rooms. Nothing worth stealing. Except my side. The only part that still had value. The only place that looked lived in. That made it a target. Mitchell was helping me sell it, so I was constantly cleaning. Wiping everything down. Resetting the space over and over, like if I made it look normal enough, it would stop feeling dangerous. But it never did. Every showing meant strangers walking through a place that no longer felt safe. Every night meant listening for footsteps that didn't belong to me. I could feel the house being watched. One night, I heard it. Not voices. Not talking. Scuffling. The sound of bodies colliding where they shouldn't be. I walked down the hallway slowly with my shotgun in hand. My heart was already racing, and I pushed the bedroom door open. There was a man on top of one of the roommates. Fists flying. Rage spilling out of him in broken sentences. Demanding money. Demanding something that didn't exist. The room felt small. Claustrophobic. Like it was closing in. I didn't think. I reacted. I grabbed him by the hair and pulled him off. Threw him out onto the porch hard enough that he hit the ground and scrambled like an animal cornered. I slapped him in the face with the butt of my gun. He stared at me unfazed with a look like he wanted to peel the flesh off my bones. My shotgun was in my hands. It felt heavy. Familiar. Necessary. He didn't care. That was the scariest part. He looked at me like the weapon meant nothing. Like desperation had already burned through whatever fear was supposed to live there. I raised it straight up in the air and fired it once into the night. The sound tore through the air and vanished into the trees. For a split second, everything went silent. Then he ran. As fast as he could. Down the driveway. Into the moonlit sky. Gone. Scurrying down the driveway like a zombie that should never have been there. I stood there shaking. The porch light buzzing. The house behind me was breathing as it had just exhaled. That was it. That was the last night. A decade complete, in Micky and Kevin's life that they never got to finish. I didn't sleep there again. That night was the end. The last time I stayed in that house. The place where I had grown up. Where I had raised my siblings. Where grief and responsibility had lived longer than they should have. I left knowing one thing for sure. That house had taken everything it was going to take from me. And I was done letting it.

The house sat exactly where it always had, hidden deep in the trees like it had learned how to disappear. Moss clung to the roof. Wet leaves pressed into the deck as if they had been there for years. The forest wrapped around it from every direction, quiet and

unmoving, the kind of silence that settles into your chest and stays there. It never felt like a house. It felt like responsibility. The chimney still leaned the same way it always had. The wood siding was darker now, swollen from rain and winters that never seemed to end. The windows reflected trees instead of sky, like the place had stopped looking outward a long time ago. It had learned how to turn inward. How to hold pain without letting it spill.

This was where I came back at twenty-four years old after my parents died. I remember pulling into the driveway that first night with a car full of boxes and a grief so heavy I could barely breathe through it. Overnight, everything changed. I stopped being just a kid myself and became the one who had to hold everything together. I raised my siblings here. This house watched me become someone else. Someone heavier. Someone older than his age. I learned how to survive here. How to wake up every day and keep moving, even when I did not want to exist inside my own body. I learned how to pay bills, fix things that broke, make food when nothing felt appetizing, and stay calm when panic lived in my throat. I learned how to be strong because there was no alternative. Every room holds a version of me that no longer exists. The living room where grief sat with us like another person. The kitchen where I learned how to stretch what little we had. The hallway where I stood alone at night, listening to the house breathe, terrified of what would happen if I failed. This place absorbed everything. The anger. The fear. The exhaustion. The nights I cried alone because I did not think I was enough. The mornings I stood in front of the mirror, trying to convince myself I could keep going. Ten years.

Ten years of putting my life on hold. Ten years of carrying a responsibility that was never supposed to be mine. Ten years of finishing a life my parents never got the chance to finish.

And now the U-Haul sat in the driveway, bright and out of place against the trees. The last thing that would ever leave this house was me.

I walked through the rooms one final time. My footsteps sounded louder than they ever had. Every creak felt like a goodbye. I ran my hand along the walls, the doorframes, the places where time had worn the wood smooth. I could almost hear my parents' voices, like echoes trapped inside the grain.

Outside, the forest stood still. No wind. No birds. Even the trees seemed to understand what was happening. I thought I wanted this day more than anything. For years, I told myself that leaving would feel like freedom. Like relief. Like the end of something painful. Instead, it felt like tearing myself out by the roots. Standing there with the keys in my hand, I realized I was not just leaving a house. I was leaving the version of myself who learned how to survive here. I was leaving the boy who carried everyone else before he ever learned how to carry himself. I was letting go of a decade of hurt, pain, memories, and ghosts. Micky, the day you died, you told me what I had to do.

It took me ten years. It was not easy. It cost me pieces of myself I will never get back. But I did it. When I closed the door for the last time, the sound echoed longer than it should have. Then the forest swallowed it whole. The house stood there quietly, holding everything I could not take it with me. I walked away carrying the rest. I wasn't perfect. I made mistakes. But I succeeded in a situation where anyone else would have failed. I looked to the sky and thought to myself, I hope you and Kevin are looking down, proud of me. That was the end of it. That decade was over. My twenties were gone and part of my thirties, sealed inside those walls, buried under pine needles and rain. Ten years disappeared the moment I turned the key for the last time. I stepped out of that house older than I should have been, carrying a life I never planned to live, and suddenly, there was nothing behind me to return to.

I was in my thirties now. A fresh start, people like to call it. Starting over. A new chapter. But standing there in the quiet, it did not yet feel like freedom. It felt like walking forward without a map. Like stepping into open air and hoping the ground would appear beneath my feet. Back to Medford I went.

13

A NEW LIFE

When I moved back to Medford, I went back to doing what I knew how to do.

Not because it worked. Because it was familiar. I had money from the house. A good chunk. Enough that I should have felt secure. Enough that I should have been able to settle somewhere and breathe. Instead, I drifted. I rented rooms from whoever had one open. Friends. Acquaintances. Anyone who said yes. Every place started the same. Polite conversations. Smiles. Assurances. And every place ended the same way. Disaster. The first woman seemed normal at first. Quiet. Friendly. The kind of person who talked about God and routine. Then I found out she was a biker. Selling drugs out of the house. Coke. And other things. People I didn't know were coming and going at all hours. I didn't argue. I didn't negotiate. I packed and left. She was furious that I didn't give her thirty days' notice. I didn't care.

I wasn't bringing my kids around drugs. No lease, no deposit. My kids mattered more to me than anything. I walked away and didn't look back. The second house lasted longer. It felt calmer. Safe enough. Until one of her dogs bit one of my five-year-old sons on the mouth. Nine stitches. Everything blew up after that. Shock. Yelling. Accusations. Chaos. We're friends now. Time softened it. But in that moment, there was no option. I had to leave. Again. Suddenly. Scrambling. The third place was fine on paper. No drugs. No danger. No drama. It just wasn't home. I stayed two months and felt like a guest the entire time. Like I was borrowing space in someone else's life. So I left. Three moves in one year.

After being stuck in the same house for a decade, raising my siblings, carrying responsibility that never let up, it broke something in me. I felt untethered. Like I belonged nowhere. I had friends. I had money. I had kids who depended on me. But I didn't have a home.

Then finally, I did. I found a place that was mine. I had joint custody of the twins, and had them half the time at this point. No roommates. No shared spaces. No explanations. I remember standing in the empty living room after moving everything in. Boxes everywhere. Muscles aching. Exhausted in a way sleep couldn't fix. And still, I felt proud. I had worked for it. Fought for it. Earned it. It wasn't easy. Nothing ever was. But it was real. For the first time in a long time, I felt like I had planted my feet somewhere. Around the same time, I got my first professional job. The ER. A hospital. A badge. A schedule. A role that mattered. I felt legitimate. Like I had crossed some invisible line. I was helping people on the worst days of their lives. I took it seriously. I showed up early. I worked hard. I wore the badge like proof that I was finally building something stable. For nine months, it felt right. Then one afternoon, they called my name. Not over the intercom. Quietly. A supervisor told me the manager wanted to see me. No reason given. No tone. Just a look that made my stomach drop before my mind could catch up. The door closed behind me. She didn't ask how I was. She didn't ask questions at all. She leaned forward and told me I was high on marijuana at work. Said it like a conclusion. Like a verdict that had already been reached. I laughed at first. Not because it was funny. Because my body didn't know what else to do. She said she could smell it on me. I told her that was impossible. I told her I was sober. I told her I had kids. I told her I would never do that. Each sentence felt smaller than the last. Each word vanished into the air between us.

Her voice got louder. She started slamming papers onto the desk. Throwing them at me like evidence.

Telling me to resign. Over and over. Saying it would be easier if I just resigned. That this would all go away if I signed something and left.

I refused. That's when time stopped behaving normally. She kept me in that office. Minutes lost meaning. The air felt thick. The walls felt closer every time she raised her voice. My heart was pounding so hard I could feel it in my throat. She didn't stop. She talked at me, over me, through me. Accusations were stacking on top of each. I couldn't tell where one ended and the next began. I felt my body slipping into something old. Something familiar. That trapped panic. That nowhere-to-go terror I thought I had left behind years earlier. Then they moved me. Not home. A patient room. They put me in a bed like I was the one being evaluated. Told me to wait. Closed the door. I sat there shaking, listening to the ER continue outside like nothing had happened. Like I hadn't just been erased. I asked if I could leave.

They told me that if I drove home, they would call the police and have me arrested for a DUI. My mind short-circuited. I was sober. I knew I was sober. But suddenly reality didn't matter. Authority did. I thought about my kids. About losing everything over something that wasn't even real. Eventually, they drug tested me. No apology. No explanation. They took my badge. Security came. That walk out of the ER is still burned into my nervous system. They didn't rush it. They walked me slowly down the hallway like I was heading to jail. Nurses stopped what they were doing. Doctors watched through the glass. People I worked beside. People I trusted. People who had no idea what was happening but were watching it anyway. I felt naked. I felt like a criminal. I felt small. The doors opened and closed behind me, and just like that, I was outside. No badge. No job. No dignity. Then they made me wait.

Seventeen days. Seventeen days of silence. No answers. No results. No closure. Just the replay. Over and over. Her voice. The room. The threat. The walk. When the test finally came back clean, nothing was fixed.

They wouldn't show it to me. They didn't apologize. I made a post about the whole experience. It went viral, with thousands of shares. It got back to them, and they sent someone from Portland. High-level HR. Calm voice. Soft words. Damage control. They asked when I wanted to come back to work. That was it. No acknowledgment of what they had done. No recognition of the trauma they caused. Just a quiet attempt to pretend it never happened. Something broke in me that day. I never felt safe there again. I never trusted authority the same way. Every time a door closed behind me, my chest tightened. Every raised voice made my body brace for impact. That moment didn't just humiliate me. It rewired me. I worked there for the next 6 years and I should have walked away that day.

2020 hit, and COVID didn't arrive like a disaster in a movie. COVID didn't just empty streets. It emptied its meaning. Everyone was locked inside with nothing but their phones, their fear, and an algorithm that suddenly had more power than any institution. Attention became the only thing still moving. And some people learned how to catch it while it was airborne. Dusty was one of them. While the world spiraled, he sat in front of his phone and treated the entire moment like satire. Calm. Deadpan. Unbothered. He understood something early that most people missed. In chaos, people don't want the truth. They want certainty or confusion. He gave them both. TikTok, his name was Dustin Tyler. His account to this day is @omfgitsdustintyler. Every single night, he went live at 9:30 PM CST. No excuses. No breaks. No mystery about the schedule. That consistency turned into a ritual. He told stories with a straight face that were obviously impossible if you thought about them for more than a second. He said he was Keanu Reeves' son. He implied connections to celebrities he had never met. He never confirmed. Never denied. Just let the internet argue with itself. That confusion was the hook. Comments exploded. People fought in real time. Some believed him. Some were furious at anyone who did. Some laughed and stayed anyway. The algorithm didn't care why they stayed. It only cared that they did. The numbers climbed faster than any of us could process. Two million followers. Thirty-nine million likes. While the rest of us were figuring out how to survive lockdowns, Dusty figured out how to scale attention. He made more money than all of us. Not quietly. Not accidentally. Publicly. Repeatedly. Night after night, thousands of people planned their evenings around his livestream. Google his name now and it's all there. Articles. Videos. Debates. That's not a character. That's really him. Watching it happen in real time felt unreal. Of course, I tried it too. Everyone did. I leaned into satire from a different angle. I said I was a grown-up Disney child star. Played it straight. Let people argue about which show I was on. A couple of videos took off. Millions of views. Two hundred thousand followers almost overnight. Then the internet leaked into real life. I took my son to Universal Studios. Just a normal day. Heat. Lines. Popcorn. And people started staring too long. Whispering. Then someone asked if it was really me. Asked for a picture. Asked for an autograph. It happened more than once. Standing there with my kid, Sharpie in my hand, I realized how thin the wall was between anonymity and recognition. How arbitrary it all was. How fast a joke could turn into a crowd. But I also saw the difference. Dusty committed. He showed up every night like it was church. Same energy. Same refusal to explain himself. He treated the algorithm like a stage and the audience like collaborators in the illusion. While people chased fame, he built routine. While others argued about truth, he let ambiguity do the work. That's how it happened. Not because he was the most talented. Not because he was the loudest. Because he understood timing. COVID cracked the world open. Attention spilled everywhere. Most of it evaporated. Some of it pooled. And Dusty stepped directly into it without flinching. Fame didn't look like red carpets or billboards. It looked like a phone propped up on a counter while the world watched from their couches, desperate for something that felt alive. Some people survived COVID by hiding. Some people reinvented themselves. Dustin Tyler became unavoidable by treating the whole thing like a joke and never blinking when it worked.

My first day working in the ER during COVID, I pulled into the hospital parking lot and almost turned around because I thought I was in the wrong place. A massive white plastic tent had been erected outside, stretching across the asphalt like a temporary border crossing. Signs everywhere. Arrows. Warnings. Masks required. Screening this way. And no one. The tent was empty. I walked through it anyway, my footsteps loud, the plastic walls snapping slightly in the wind. Hand sanitizer stations stood like sentries, untouched. Clipboards waited for names that never came. Inside the ER, it was worse. Nothing. No gurneys in the hallway. No coughing. No shouting. No chaos. Just fluorescent lights humming over empty beds. The kind of quiet you only hear at three in the morning, except it was the middle of the day. Upstairs, the same thing. Entire floors vacant. Nurses standing around with nowhere to go. Doctors checking phones. Everyone waiting for something that never showed up. Meanwhile, the TV in the corner screamed catastrophe. Death counters. Red maps. Breaking news banners that never stopped breaking. Hospitals overflowing. Systems collapsing. And I would look around at my actual reality and feel like I had slipped into the wrong timeline. Then the world shut down. Not slowly. Instantly. Gyms closed overnight. Stores boarded up. Restaurants went dark. Roads emptied. The city folded in on itself. Oregon turned into a ghost town. Stay home. Stay safe. Don't gather. Don't touch. Six feet apart. Don't breathe near each other. People obeyed. We sat inside our houses watching the same news loop over and over. Numbers climbing. Fear thickening. Every cough felt like a threat. Every stranger felt radioactive. Time blurred. Days lost their names. Life shrank down to couches, screens, and silence. In healthcare, the pressure shifted. Not patients. Control. Emails. Meetings. Policies changing weekly. Then daily. Then hourly. Protocols stacked on protocols. Signs taped over signs. They literally made up everything as they went along, having no idea what they were doing. Then the word that changed everything. Vaccines. They came fast. Too fast for my comfort. And they were pushed harder than anything I had ever seen in medicine. Not discussed. Not debated. Pushed. Lotteries, Posters. Emails. Mandatory trainings. Tone sharpening by the week. Then the ultimatum. Get the shot or lose your job. No nuance. No room. No conversation. I worked in the ER. I had shown up every day while the world hid. I had walked through that empty hospital when everyone else was home watching fear on television. And now I was being told that none of that mattered unless I complied. I didn't trust it. Not because I was reckless. Because I was paying attention. The pressure felt wrong. The speed felt wrong. The certainty felt manufactured. And the harder they pushed, the more my instincts screamed. I refused. I made peace with walking away. With unemployment. With starting over. I watched another hospital across town fire staff in waves for non-compliance. Good doctors, Good nurses. Good techs. Gone overnight. Years erased with an email. I filed exemption after exemption. Religious. Ethical. Personal. I fought quietly but relentlessly. Every denial felt like a countdown. Every approval delay felt like standing on a trapdoor. Then one day, it went through. Approved. I sat in my car afterward and just breathed. Relief mixed with survivor's guilt. I kept my job while people around me lost everything. Not because they were bad providers. Not because they were dangerous. Because they refused. Outside of work, life stayed frozen. No gym. No routine. No release. My body went soft. My mind went restless. We stayed home and watched TV because there was nothing else to do. Streets stayed empty. Businesses disappeared. Friendships faded into screens. The world felt smaller, meaner, and tightly wound. COVID didn't feel like a plague where I stood it. It felt like control. It felt like a test. Of fear. Of obedience. Of who you were when the pressure came from every direction at once. Someday, people will talk about it casually. Like weather. Like history. But living through it felt like standing in a hospital that should have been full and wasn't. Watching a world panic while everything around you went eerily quiet. Knowing something fundamental had shifted, knowing it was all a lie, even if no one could quite explain why. That was COVID. Not just sickness. Control. Silence. And the unsettling realization that reality and narrative do not always match. I loved the ER. Not in a heroic way. Not in the way people say it when they want to sound important. I loved it because it felt real. Immediate. Necessary. When you walked through those doors, nothing was theoretical anymore. Everything mattered right now. I worked directly under doctors. Not observing. Not standing in the corner. I was in it. Hands where they were needed. Moving when someone yelled my name. Doing things that actually changed outcomes. I went to codes. Real ones. People who were dead when I got there. Skin blue. Lips purple. No pulse. No breath. Bodies that felt heavy and wrong under my hands. I climbed up on the bed and compressed their chest over and over and over. Counting. Locking my elbows. Feeling ribs shift beneath me. Sweat dripping. Arms burning. No music. No drama. Just the sound of compressions and the clock ticking down their life. Sometimes they came back. A gasp. A twitch. A pulse returning under someone's fingers. Color slowly creeping back where there had been none. Those moments stayed with me. Not like miracles. Like proof that what I was doing mattered. I was good at it. Good enough that a nurse pulled me aside one day and told me I should be recognized. She said I had some of the strongest, cleanest CPR she had ever seen. That I had helped bring multiple patients back. I saw things most people never do. Gunshot wounds. Mangled limbs. Accidents that erased pieces of people in seconds. Blood everywhere. Screams. Silence. I did legal blood draws for DUI cases with police watching my hands like hawks. I learned how to stay calm when everything was chaos and how to move fast without panicking. It grounded me. By then, I was in my mid-thirties. Still me. Still capable of going out. Still capable of chaos if I wanted it. But something had shifted. The two lives I used to live were no longer equal. There was a time when I split myself in half. Father on one side. Party animal on the other. Nights out. Women. Noise. Then mornings with kids. School. Responsibility. I ran both lives hard for a long time. But eventually, one of them stopped calling as loudly. I drifted. Not dramatically. Quietly. Weekends stopped being about where I was going and started being about who I was with. Baseball games. Movie theaters. Popcorn and sticky floors. Sitting in bleachers with my kids while the sun went down. Taking them to do things that would stick in their memory, even if they never said it out loud. Every weekend became theirs. I built my life around them. Their schedules. Their moods. Their laughter. I didn't feel like I was giving anything up. I felt like I was finally where I was supposed to be. Sure, once in a while I'd go out. Once in a while, I'd hook up with someone. But it wasn't my identity anymore. It wasn't my fuel. It didn't define me. Fatherhood did. My kids took up my entire life and I let them. Gladly. They were my purpose. The thing that anchored me when everything else felt unstable. When work was hard. When the world felt loud. When the past tried to pull me back into old versions of myself. At some point, without announcing it, I stopped being a man who happened to have kids. I became a father. And that was enough. I didn't lose my faith all at once. It bled out slowly the day Micky decided to trust God more than the doctors. Micky believed with everything she had. The kind of belief that didn't question, didn't hedge, didn't leave room for doubt. When they told her surgery could save her, she shook her head. She said God would heal her. She said it with certainty. Calm. Peaceful. Like the decision had already been made somewhere higher than us. Gideon enforced this delusion every single day she was on this earth until the end. I wanted to believe her. I watched her pray instead of consent. I watched time pass while hope stood still. I watched her body fail while faith stayed firm. And when she died anyway, something inside me broke clean in half. I didn't rage at God. I went quiet. I stopped talking to Him. Stopped listening. Stopped asking. If this was what faith did, if belief could kill the person who trusted it most, then I wanted no part of it. I carried that resentment for years. Let it harden. Let it turn into distance. I lived my life without Him and told myself I was fine. Then life kept happening. Pain stacked up. Loss piled on loss. I survived things I should not have. I helped save lives. I raised children. I held death in my hands and watched people come back from it. And somewhere in the silence between all of that, the question returned. Not why did you take her? But why am I still here? I didn't come back to God through certainty. I came back through exhaustion. The day of the baptism, my hands were shaking. Not from fear. From weight. Years of it. Guilt. Anger. Regret. Everything I never processed because I was too busy surviving. The room was quiet in that way churches get when something important is about to happen. The water waited. Still. Reflective. Honest. When I stepped in, my heart was beating so hard I thought everyone could hear it. The pastor took my hand. He looked at me, not at the crowd, not at the room. At me. Like he was seeing the version of myself I never showed anyone. He started speaking and it felt like the words were being pulled straight out of my chest. He named everything. The pain. The heartbreak. The loss. The guilt. The anger. He said I had been carrying it all for too long. That I wasn't meant to hold it by myself. That it was time to let it go. Not forget it. Not erase it. But release it. That this was a beginning. I felt it then. Something cracking open. My eyes burned. My chest tightened. Tears came fast and uncontrollable, the kind you don't try to stop because stopping would hurt worse. I felt the weight start to lift, not dramatically, not all at once, but enough to know it was real. When he lowered me into the water, everything went quiet. No thoughts. No memories. No arguments with God. Just water closing over my ears and the strange peace of surrender. For a second, I was nowhere. Then I came back up, gasping, blinking, soaked, exposed. And lighter. I didn't hear angels. I didn't see visions. But I felt something I hadn't felt since before my mother died. Peace. Not answers. Not explanations. Peace. I walked out of that water knowing my faith wasn't the same as it used to be. It was scarred. Complicated. Earned the hard way. But it was mine again. And for the first time in a long time, I felt like I wasn't carrying everything alone. That was the moment I found my faith back. Not because God saved her. But because He didn't abandon me when I stopped believing.

14

DATING ON FIRE

MEDFORD DID SOMETHING TO people. I didn't understand it at first. I just knew that no matter how carefully I showed up, no matter how normal I tried to be, the same kind of chaos kept finding me.

Over and over. I was dating a lot then. Not in a reckless way. I was trying. Going on real dates. Showing up on time. Wanting something that made sense. Wanted to settle down, and every time, something would crack open that made me stop and think, What the fuck is happening here? One girl I really liked, we went out for dinner. First date. Nervous energy. That moment where you start imagining what the next few weeks could look like. Halfway through, she leaned in and told me, very casually, that one night she got too drunk, taking shots with her brother, and slept with him. She said it casually, as if she were telling me she missed an exit on the freeway. Casual in conversation, like picking an appetizer. I remember the room going quiet. The sound of silverware. People laughing in the background. Me sitting there, trying to figure out how a sentence like that exists in the world, let alone on a first date. Another girl came into my life fast. We hit it off. Texting. Laughing. Easy. I worked a lot back then. Late nights. Long shifts. I didn't text for a day. Maybe two. At seven in the morning, after I had worked until two a.m. I slept maybe three hours. I woke up to someone slamming their body into my front door, banging. Screaming. Kicking. I stumbled out of bed, heart racing, convinced something terrible was happening. When I looked through the window, it was her. Eyes wild. Hair red and a mess that matched her face. Shouting my name like I'd committed some unforgivable crime. I didn't even have time to process it before she started calling my work, trying to tell them I was posting her medical chart online. Something completely fabricated. Something that could have destroyed my career. I remember standing in my kitchen afterward, phone in my hand, realizing how close chaos could get without warning.

Then there was the pool date. It was supposed to be simple. A YMCA pool. Her kid. My kids. A normal afternoon.

Something almost wholesome. She texted me that her tire blew out on the way and she had to go buy new ones.

So I showed up anyway. And sitting ten feet away from me, watching our kids swim, was her child's father. A man she wasn't with anymore. A man who had no idea who I was. No idea that I was supposed to be there with her.

I spent the afternoon making small talk with him, sitting on a bench, pretending this was normal. Pretending I wasn't on a date with her baby daddy. Another woman liked to meet me at the gym. Or at least she liked the idea of it. She would say she was on her way. I'd be there. Waiting. Stretching. Checking the clock. Then nothing. Later that night, always late, always after I'd already accepted it, she'd text that she had to fly to Montana to help her mom. Emergencies that only existed at the exact moment she was supposed to show up. It kept happening. Different faces. Same energy. Same confusion.

And then there was the one that hurt the most. She was my best friend. That's what she was before anything else. We talked every day. We knew each other's stories. She felt safe. Familiar. Like someone I could finally stop bracing around. She watched my kids, and she meant the world to me.

We hooked up once, and she went down on me, just once. And I let myself believe maybe this was the one that would turn into something real.

Not long after, she started dating another guy. She ghosted me for a alcoholic guy who hit her and pulled out her hair. I remember sitting with that realization, staring at my phone, feeling something twist in my chest. I had a job. Stability. No record. No chaos. No threats. No fists. And somehow, in that town, that made me the wrong choice. I started to understand then. It wasn't that I was unlucky. It wasn't that I was bad at dating. It was that I was trying to build something solid in a place that thrived on damage. Medford didn't want stability. It didn't want calm. It wanted familiar pain. And I kept walking straight into it, wondering why nothing ever held. The most unsettling thing about that town was the sheer amount of cousin fucking that went on there.

I have stories that still make people stare at me like I'm lying. But this one still takes the cake. I met her online. One of those late-night conversations that turns into a real address faster than it should. I went to her house on Thanksgiving. Late. She made me a plate of Thanksgiving dinner at night like it was nothing. We hung out a few times after that. No sex. Just kissing. Talking. Normal. Almost sweet.

Eventually, we decided to go on an actual date. Dinner was fine. Easy. We talked. Laughed. Nothing felt off. Afterward, we went downtown to get drinks. That's when it shifted.

She kept drinking. One drink turned into another, then another. I stayed mostly sober. Just a light buzz. Enough to notice that she was slipping.

At some point, in the middle of our date, she wandered over to two bald guys in their forties and started flirting with them. Hard. Laughing. Touching arms. Letting them buy her drinks. I watched from a distance, not angry, just confused. Then concerned.

She was drunk enough that she almost went home with them. I stopped it. Not because I was jealous, but because it didn't feel right. She could

barely stand. I didn't trust those guys. I didn't trust the situation. So she came back to my place. Nothing happened. She climbed into my bed and passed out almost immediately. Then, it happened. Projectile vomiting. Everywhere. My bed. My chest. The floor. It was like something out of a horror movie. Just endless.

She passed out again. I cleaned everything. The bed. The floor. Her. Me. I stripped the sheets, wiped

everything down, and tried to salvage the night. I lay back down, exhausted.

Then, she did it again. More vomit. Worse this time. She rolled onto the floor, still throwing up. At that point, I gave up on sleep. I grabbed a metal bowl from the kitchen and slid it under her head. A few seconds later, I heard a loud clunk. I looked down into the bowl.

Two full sets of dentures. Top and bottom. I had no idea. I just stared for a second, stunned. Then my medical brain kicked in. I went to the bathroom, put on a glove, rinsed them off, and gently put them back in her mouth so she wouldn't wake up mortified.

Earlier, she had fallen off the bed and hit her head on my nightstand, splitting it open a little. I checked her pupils. Made sure she was breathing. Made sure she was safe. She went back to sleep. And somehow, after all of that, she's still one of my best friends to this day. It didn't stop. It just kept happening. Over and over and over again. I'd meet someone, and if they were broken, if there was something wrong beneath the surface, I could see it immediately. Most people ran from that kind of pain. I leaned toward it.

I didn't fall in love with who they were. I fell in love with the hurt inside them. The parts they didn't talk about. The damage they carried quietly. I could recognize it because it lived in me too.

And every time, I told myself this one would be different. I kept trying.

No matter how many times it went sideways, no matter how much it cost me, I kept trying. I'd convince myself that if I just loved harder, stayed longer, understood more, it would eventually work. Instead, it broke me a little more each time. My PTSD got worse. My anxiety sharpened. My depression sank deeper. Every relationship didn't heal me. It reopened things I had spent years trying to hold together. I started to feel cursed. Like I wasn't meant to end up with anyone. Like the universe kept showing me the same lesson in different bodies, daring me to figure it out. But I didn't stop. I wanted a future like the one I was supposed to have

with Tayla before everything collapsed.

I wanted to try again. Carefully. Honestly. I wanted something real.

There was always something. Mental illness. Drugs. Another guy. Chaos calling louder than stability. Pain choosing familiarity over safety.

Every time, they chose something else.

I was never chosen. I could be patient. Loyal. Present. Sober. Safe. I could show up every day. I could offer a life that didn't explode. And somehow, that was never enough. Eventually, I stopped asking what was wrong with them and started asking what was

wrong with me. Why I kept loving people who couldn't stay. Why I kept reaching for fire and calling it warmth. Why being steady made me invisible. That's when it started to click. I wasn't chasing love. I was chasing redemption. Trying to prove that if I could save someone else, maybe I'd finally be worth saving too.

And that realization scared me more than being alone ever did.

Then suddenly, I wasn't alone. The first thing you notice is the color, Green does not belong here. Not in a hospital parking lot on my truck that smells like hot asphalt, bleach, and burnt coffee. Not under fluorescent lights that buzz like dying insects. Not in a world of gray scrubs, gray concrete, gray mornings that blur together until you forget what day it is. But there it is. A rose. Green. Artificial. Perfect. Folded too neatly to be natural, like it was made by hands that wanted control more than beauty.

It's sitting on your truck like it has always been there. Like it knows the place better than you do. Your fingers hesitate before touching it. That quiet moment stretches, the way it does right before something bad happens. The steering wheel is still warm from the sun. Your reflection stares back from the windshield, tired eyes, jaw tight, tattoos crawling up your hand like warnings you forgot to read. You pick it up. It feels wrong. Too clean. Too deliberate. That night, your phone lights up. "Want to know a secret?" You scroll back through messages you never opened. Hundreds of them back, one you ignored. Little gray bubbles stacking up like unanswered prayers. Sixteen days earlier, one stands out. "I see you. Nice green scrubs." Your stomach drops. Because you never told anyone where you worked. And then she sends the video. Another rose. Identical. Same shade of green. Same tight folds. Held in a hand you do not recognize, filmed too close, too intimate, like she wants you to notice the texture. Like she wants you to know she

touched it before you did. "I know where you are." You laugh it off online. Joke about milk cartons. About becoming a lampshade. Humor as armor. People react. People comment. People think it's funny.

You do not. Because a few days later, you go out to your truck on break, and the air feels heavier. Like the parking

lot is holding its breath. There is a note this time. Another rose. Always green. Army green the same color as your truck. The paper is plain. The handwriting uneven. Pressed hard, like she was angry when she wrote it. Manic or excited. "I saw the post you made about the rose. You think blocking me will get rid of me? I may not have met you, but I love you, and you WILL be mine!!! I'm gonna try even harder now. Just know I always know where you are."

Your pulse is loud in your ears. You read it again. Slower this time. "I always know where you are." You look around the cab. The passenger seat. The mirrors. The dark tint of the windows. Nothing moves, but the feeling does not leave. It crawls up your spine and settles between your shoulders like a hand that refuses to let go. You tell yourself it's nothing. You tell yourself people are weird. You tell yourself this is just some lonely person who got carried away. Then it escalates. Lunch break. You look in the back of your truck and there they are. Brand new nursing shoes. Still boxed. Still tagged. One hundred and sixty dollars worth of precision comfort you never asked for. Sitting there like an offering. Like proof. You post about it. You joke again. People laugh again. At the same time you don't miss what it means. She was here. She touched your truck. She knew which size you wear. That night, the parking lot feels different. Every shadow looks intentional. Every sound feels closer than it should. Tires crunch on gravel, and you flinch before you can stop yourself. You start checking behind you when you walk. You start locking doors twice. Green shows up everywhere now. In your thoughts. In your dreams. In the corner of your vision when you are sure nothing is there. And then the truth hits you, not all at once, but in pieces that refuse to stay quiet. She knew your scrubs were green before the rose ever appeared. She knew your schedule. She knew your truck. She did not need to guess.

Because this was never random. This was someone who watched you long before you noticed her. Someone who didn't need a response from you. Someone who already decided how the story ends. The reveal is not dramatic. No mask comes off. No confrontation. Just a name you recognize too late. A woman from months ago. A face you ignored. A message request you never answered because she "wasn't your type."

But you were hers. From the moment she saw you. And that is the scariest part. Not that she found you. Not that she followed you. Not even that she left proof. It's the certainty in her words. The calm confidence. The promise. "I always know where you are." The camera would pull back here. Wide shot. You standing alone in the parking lot under flickering lights, clutching a green rose like evidence you cannot unsee.

The music drops low. Unsettling. Slow. Because you realize something that makes your chest tighten. This is not over.

This is just the part where you finally understand you were never alone. Then the calls started. At first, it was almost quiet. One text. Two. The phone lighting up on the nightstand like a pulse. You told yourself it was nothing. You turned it face down. You slept. By morning, there were ten. By night, fifty. Then one morning you woke up, and your phone felt heavier than it should. Seventy missed calls. The screen hot in your hand. Numbers stacking on top of each other like they were fighting for space.

You scrolled. "I miss you." "Why won't you answer?" "I know you're awake." "I see your light on." The next night it was eighty. The next night, one hundred. Your ringtone stopped sounding like a sound and started sounding like a threat. You stopped sleeping

with the phone on. You stopped charging it next to your bed. You started putting it across the room like distance could help.

It didn't. That's when you noticed the car.

Late. Always late. Headlights slowly rolling past your house. No music. No hurry. Just enough speed to say this isn't an accident. The engine noise lingered too long. You would stand in the dark and watch it disappear, heart hammering, telling yourself it was just someone lost. Then your phone would buzz. "I see you." The first time you were in the kitchen. Shirt off. Cooking. Steam rising from the pan. The window was black like a mirror. You froze when the message came in. "I see you through the kitchen window, nice chest tattoo." Your chest went cold. Another night, you were outside, flipping chicken on the grill. Summer air. Fire popping. Smoke clinging to your skin. You felt exposed without knowing why. Your phone vibrated.

"I see you." " Nice haircut." You dropped the tongs. You started closing curtains. Locking doors. Turning lights off. You started living as if the house itself were watching you. You stopped bringing anyone over. Except you didn't stop dating. And that's when it got worse. She found her. The girl you were seeing started acting strange. Checking mirrors. Taking different routes home.

Locking herself inside and crying without knowing why. Until one night she called you, shaking, voice breaking apart mid-sentence.

"There's a car outside my house. It's been there for an hour." You already knew.

She started following her. Sitting across the street. Watching. Waiting. Standing too close in grocery stores. Appearing where she shouldn't be. Leaving no proof except the fear that lingered after. And then one night, it stopped being subtle. You came home late. The house was dark. Too dark. The porch light was off. The door was unlocked. You felt it immediately. That wrongness in the air. Like the house had been disturbed. Like someone else's breath was still inside it. You stepped in. The door slammed behind you. She came out of the hallway smiling. Too calm. Too close. Her eyes were wide. Shining. Unblinking. She smelled like sweat and perfume and beef tacos with something sour underneath it.

You backed up. She moved forward. Her hand flashed. Something metal caught the light. A blade. Small but sharp. Shaking, but not enough. Your heart slammed so hard it hurt. She lunged. She ended up holding you against the wall with the blade to your throat. Suddenly, everything exploded at once. Furniture crashing. Your head hitting the wall. Her screaming your name like it was love and hate tangled together. The knife slashed the air inches from your skin. You shoved her back. She stumbled, fell, and came up feral. "I CAN'T LOSE YOU!" You ran. Barefoot. Door open. Night air tearing into your lungs. She chases you. Screaming your name like a banshee screaming out of hell. Footsteps pounding. Neighbors' lights flickering on like startled eyes. You didn't look back. You vaulted the fence. Cut your arm. Felt it tear. Kept going. Sirens howled somewhere close. Or maybe they were in your head. She tripped. Fell hard, her ankle snapped, and a bone protruded out. The knife skittered across concrete.

Police lights washed the street in red and blue sirens that feel like a dream. They tackle her, then tasered her, immediately after. She fights like an animal. She urinates in her pants. Spitting. Crying. Laughing. Screaming your name over and over until it didn't sound like a name anymore. They took her away in cuffs.

Still smiling. Weeks later, you heard where she ended up. Not jail. A locked ward. White walls. No mirrors. No phones. No windows that open, padded walls. They said words like fixation, delusion, and danger to self and others. You stand in your house afterward, bandaged, shaking, staring at the windows. Green was gone. But you still close the curtains. Because some things don't leave when the threat does. They stay in your head in silence.

15

AMSTERDAM DREAMS

THIRTY-FIVE YEARS OLD. THAT'S when it finally hit. The mirror didn't lie anymore. The hairline had been retreating for years, slow enough to ignore if you wanted to. Most men do. They shrug. They cope. They let time win. I'm not most men. I researched quietly for years. Forums. Before and after photos. Clinics. Surgeons. Statistics. In the United States, it was sixteen thousand dollars for sixteen hundred grafts. A number so insulting it almost felt personal. Everyone kept saying the same word. Turkey. The hair transplant capital of the world. I spent two years narrowing it down. Not guesses. Not shortcuts. The best clinic. The best surgeon. When I finally booked it, it felt surreal. Three thousand dollars. Unlimited grafts. Five-star hotel. Limo service to and from the hospital.

A full transformation for less than a used car. Everyone in my life told me I was insane. I had never left the United States before. I had just gotten my passport. I was going to Istanbul alone. They warned me. Repeatedly. Don't do it. That's dangerous. Why would you go by yourself? I went anyway. Twenty-seven hours of flights, layovers, waiting, staring at departure boards in places I couldn't pronounce. By the time I landed, my body had no idea what time it was. I checked into the hotel and realized I had arrived five days before my surgery. Five days to wander. Turkey hit different. The first thing you notice is the sound. Sirens everywhere. Not emergency sirens. Calls. Big speakers mounted on towers and rooftops. Ten or twelve times a day, the city stops to listen to a man singing prayers that echo through the streets. The first one comes at five in the morning. That's how you wake up.

Not an alarm. A voice, singing in a shrill Muslim voice, words I did not understand. It was haunting. Beautiful. Disorienting. I walked for hours every day. The city felt ancient and alive at the same time. Massive mosques rose out of the skyline like something built to outlast everything else. Stone, arches, history pressed into every corner. And everywhere you looked, you could tell why people were there. Men walking around with fresh hairlines dotted in red, heads wrapped, eyes tired but hopeful. Women with bandages on their noses, swollen faces, eyes bright like they knew something new was coming. Everyone healing. Everyone waiting to become someone else. I wandered into an endless indoor bazaar. It stretched for what had to be a hundred city blocks, a maze of shops stacked on shops, gold, glass, rugs, spices, smoke, voices overlapping in every direction. I stopped at a small stall filled with glass trinkets. Bright colors. Fragile. I picked one up, and another slipped, fell, and shattered on the floor. The air changed instantly.

The shop owner snapped to attention.

"One hundred dollars American!" he shouted at me. I told him it was an accident. I would pay for the piece I broke. He stepped closer. His face hardened. "You don't come to my country and disrespect me," he said. "You pay, or you go to jail."

I turned slightly and froze. Behind me stood a soldier. Rifle pointed down but unmistakably real. I paid the hundred dollars. I didn't argue. I didn't hesitate. I just handed it over, nodded, and left as fast as I could, heart pounding, adrenaline flooding my system.

That was the moment I understood something important. I wasn't home.

And I wasn't protected. The rest of the day, I walked lighter. More alert. Bought Turkish delight from a street vendor and ate it while standing in the sun. Sweet. Sticky. Perfect. I shopped carefully after that. I picked up fake Jordans for my kids, laughed at how good the knockoffs were, and imagined them wearing them without knowing the story behind them. That was just the beginning. I was alone in a country that didn't bend for you. A place older than fear. A place where change wasn't symbolic, it was physical. And in five days, they were going to cut into my head and rebuild my reflection.

I didn't know it yet, but this trip wasn't really about hair. It was about control.

About deciding, I wasn't done becoming someone new. About proving to myself that I could walk into the unknown and not disappear. Turkey was just the doorway. Downtown Istanbul felt like stepping into a moving current. I went to see the Blue Mosque. The real one. The one you see in photos and think it has to be exaggerated. It wasn't. Thousands of people filled the courtyard, shoes stacked at the edges, voices echoing off stone that had been standing longer than most countries. Boats cut across the water nearby, packed with tourists, drifting past history

like it was scenery. I made one mistake immediately. I dressed like an American. Every two steps, someone shouted at me.

"Hey, you." "You come to my shop." "I give you good price." I said no. Two seconds later, another voice. "You come." "Good price." "Best shop."

It didn't stop. It escalated. They followed me. Not casually. Aggressively. One teenager chased me for six blocks, breathless, confused that I wouldn't stop. "But why?" he kept saying. "You come. I give you good price." I started running. They ran with me. My tattoos didn't help. My accent made it worse. Men pointed and smiled like they'd found something exotic.

"You sound like movies."

"You sound Hollywood."

"You come, Hollywood." They grabbed my arm. Tugged my sleeve. Tried to steer me into shops. One man pointed upward. "You come roof. Good view." "Come roof my shop." I genuinely thought I was about to be kidnapped. It was overwhelming. Loud. Relentless. There was no personal space, no pause, no escape. Just voices, hands, movement, pressure.

Eventually, I ducked into an underground museum just to breathe.

Roman ruins buried beneath the city. Pillars. Statues. Stone soaked in shadow and history. A Medusa head lay turned on its side at the back of the exhibit, half hidden in darkness, lit just enough to feel deliberate. Ancient. Watching. I loved it instantly.

When I was in line for the museum outside, it had been massive, but a man approached me. "I have ticket," he said. "You skip line. Fifteen dollars."

I paid him. Inside, time slowed. Cool air. Quiet footsteps. The city muffled above me. For the first time all day, my nervous system unclenched. When I finished and started up the stairs to leave, I saw him. The man who sold me the ticket. Standing at the top. Waiting.

He was scanning the crowd, as if looking for something specific. Like he hadn't expected me to come back up yet. The moment our eyes met, my stomach dropped. Every instinct I had screamed move. He stepped toward me and said something sharp in Turkish.

I didn't answer. I turned and ran straight into the crowd. Behind me, I heard him shouting. "You!" "You come here!" "You come here!" Like I had stolen something. Like I'd broken a law I didn't understand. He chased me. I didn't look back. I shoved through people, cut corners, ducked down side streets,

heart hammering in my throat until the sound of his voice finally disappeared.

That's when I called a ride. Their version of Uber pulled up in a tiny compact car. I got in shaking. The driver took off immediately. No easing into traffic. Just speed. Honking. Swerving through alleys

barely wide enough for the car. People stepped into the street without looking.

Motorbikes cut inches from our doors.

It felt like a chase scene.

He took a long route. Too long.

We weren't going toward my hotel.

My mind went straight to the worst place. Taken. Headlines. Foreign prison. Nobody knew where I was. My phone clutched in my hand, heart pounding, watching the map update slowly while the city blurred past. Finally, mercifully, the hotel appeared. I paid. Got out. Didn't look back. That night, I didn't explore. I didn't wander. I didn't push my luck.

I locked the door. Sat on the bed. Let the adrenaline drain out of me. Turkey was beautiful. Ancient. Unforgiving.

For the first time since I arrived, I understood something clearly. This trip wasn't just about changing how I looked. It was about surviving long enough to change at all. By the third night, I stopped hiding. I went to the club district. Neon soaked the streets. Bass thudded through concrete. Lines of people wrapped around doors like rituals. I paid a cover, walked into one club, drank Turkish beer, leaned against a wall and watched. Then another club. Same thing. Same noise.

Same heat. I was alone, on purpose.

That's when they found me. Two women stepped into my space like they'd already decided something.

One was tall. Blonde. Thin in a sharp, deliberate way. Fake breasts that didn't

apologize for existing. She looked sculpted. Confident. Exactly my type. The other was smaller. Dark hair. Pale skin. Softer features. Quiet eyes that watched before she moved.

Minka and Isabel. They noticed the tattoos immediately. The accent sealed it. American. Different. Interesting.

They didn't ask permission to sit close.

Hands brushed my leg. Fingers lingered on ink like they were reading it. Their English was broken. My Turkish was nonexistent. Phones came out. Translators filled the gaps. Laughter did the rest. They ordered drinks.

They leaned in. They touched without hesitation. It felt unreal. Especially after the last few days. After the fear. The chasing. The constant sense of being hunted. This was different. They kept asking me to come to their place.

I said no. I didn't trust it. Not here. Not after everything. I told them they could come to my hotel if they wanted. They looked at each other. Smiled. Agreed. Back in my room, the city noise softened. Lights low. Words mattered less. Phones stayed on the bed, glowing with half-translated jokes and dares neither language could fully explain. Truth or dare became its own language. All our clothes quickly landed on the floor. I kissed them, then they kissed each other. Then we all had sex for hours. They loved me like their bodies were starving for me. A itch they told me an American could only scratch. I remember the sun was rising, and Minka and Isabel were just lying there twitching, not able to move after the copious amount of orgasms they both endured. When it was over, there was no awkwardness. No clinging. No promises.

They dressed calmly. They both slightly limped towards the door, walking crooked, like I did my job right. A kiss on the cheek.

A smile. The door closed behind them.

I never saw either of them again.

Lying there afterward, staring at the ceiling, I realized something. For the first time since I landed in Turkey, I didn't feel afraid. I felt present.

Not because of what happened.

But because, for a moment, I stopped bracing for the next threat. I slept better that night than I had since arriving.

And when I woke up, the call to prayer echoed through the city again. Same sound. Same morning. The next morning, it was finally time. No more wandering. No more noise. No more running. A car picked me up before the city fully woke. Istanbul slid past the windows quietly this time. Mosques still. Streets calm. Like the city knew something was about to be taken from me and rebuilt. At the hospital, everything moved fast. The doctor studied my face the way an artist studies a canvas. Measured. Stepped back. Leaned in again. Then he chose a hairline. He didn't ask. He drew it.

A marker pressed against my skin. Lines traced across my forehead. Permanent intentions sketched in ink that would soon be replaced by something real. I caught my reflection and barely recognized myself.

Then they shaved my head. Every last bit. I stared at the mirror, bald, exposed, the new hairline sitting there like a promise I wasn't sure I believed yet. It felt symbolic in a way I couldn't explain. Like being stripped down to something honest. They laid me back.

That's when the needles came out. Six inches. Maybe less. Maybe more. Long enough that my brain noticed before my body could lie about it. One by one, they pierced my scalp, and lidocaine was injected deep into flesh that wasn't meant for that kind of invasion. I'm covered in tattoos. Head to toe. I know pain. This was different. Each injection felt like fire pushed under bone. My jaw locked. My hands curled. I stared at the ceiling and breathed through something that didn't want to be breathed through. Eventually, my head went numb.

That's when the work started.

Three Turkish men moved around me like a machine. No wasted motion. No small talk. Just hands, tools, precision. For six hours, they rebuilt me follicle by follicle. An assembly line of faith. Each graft placed like it mattered. Like it counted. When it was over, I was handed a mirror. I didn't look better.

I looked wrecked. Bandaged. Swollen. Red. A version of myself mid-construction. Back at the hotel, the pain arrived in waves. The back of my head leaked onto the pillow. Plasma soaked the sheets. My face swelled until it didn't feel like mine anymore. My eyes narrowed. My skin pulled tight. I

looked like I'd lost a fight with something bigger than me. They gave me ibuprofen. That was it. No narcotics. No sympathy. Just instructions and time. The nights were long. Sleep came in pieces. Every heartbeat reminded me of what I'd done. Every mirror reminded me I couldn't undo it.

A few days later, I boarded a plane home. Head wrapped. Face still swollen. Body exhausted. As the plane lifted, Istanbul shrank beneath me. It was gone, fading into clouds. A city

that had tested me, taken from me, given something back in its own brutal way. Turkey was beautiful. Turkey was hostile. Turkey was honest. I went there to change my hair. I came back changed in ways that had nothing to do with it. The next day I landed in Amsterdam. I immediately went to De Wallen, the red-light district. De Wallen didn't feel like the city, it felt like a corridor. Canals cut through the streets like black glass, breaking the red glow into jagged reflections. Windows lined both sides of the street, bodies framed behind them, still and waiting. Hundreds of faces. Hundreds of choices. Laughter spilled into the open air, mixing

with music and footsteps and water, the whole place humming like it was alive.

I walked slowly, afraid that if I stopped, I would be chosen before I chose. Across the canal, I saw her. She didn't pose or perform like the others. She just stood there, blonde hair catching the light, calm and composed, like she didn't belong on the street at all. When our eyes met, she lifted one finger and motioned me over. Casual. Certain. Like the decision had already been made. Crossing the bridge felt like crossing a line. When I went inside her building, the hallway was narrow and dark, the walls painted black, the noise of the street disappearing the moment the door closed. It felt like walking into a cave. At the end of the hall, the room itself was small and bare. A twin sized bed. Dim light. No decoration. No warmth. Up close, she was unreal. Symmetrical. Polished. The kind of beauty you expect to see on a magazine cover, not standing behind glass across a canal. She looked like a Playboy playmate dropped into the wrong world. I was terrified. My heart pounded so hard I thought she could hear it. Every sound made me tense. I kept expecting the door to open, for someone to come in, for the whole thing to turn into something dangerous. My body was there, but my mind hovered above it, detached, watching. As we started having sex, I was so nervous I couldn't perform until I did. She was moaning a language I didn't understand.

I was shaking the entire time, convinced something was about to go wrong. I felt like two men were going to burst through the door and rob me and take all my money. When it was over, the first thing I felt wasn't pleasure. It was relief. Relief that nothing terrible had happened. Relief that I could leave. When I stepped back onto the street, the red lights felt harsher. Louder. The crowd pressed in closer than before. I needed air. Distance. Something unnamed. That's when I drifted away from the main street and found the alley.

The alley felt wrong before I reached the end of it. The stones under my feet were uneven, older than the rest of the city, worn smooth in places, as if they had been walked the same way for centuries. The sound of the crowds vanished behind me, not gradually but all at once, as if someone had shut a door. Even my footsteps sounded muted, swallowed. The building was there without announcing itself. No sign. No name. Just a line of people pressed against the wall, quiet in a way that didn't match what they were waiting for. Velvet ropes guided them forward, the handles carved into penises that felt intentional, like icons. Not decoration. Instruction. A man in a tuxedo stood at the entrance, posture perfect, expression empty. He tore tickets slowly, ceremonially, like each one mattered. Like entry was permission, not purchase.

When I stepped inside, it felt like stepping into an underground carnival. The room opened wide and then closed in on itself. No windows. No sense of time. The air was heavy, sweet, and metallic at the same time. Rows of seats curved toward a stage that was already lit, already active, already in motion. There was no beginning. There was no end. The stage was lit with candles. A circular bed came out of the ground, rotating slowly in a circle. Two very attractive people were having sex on the bed, doing every position, doing everything, and doing it well. That was just the first of many things I saw. I saw things, sickening things, that I had no idea existed. I saw things that made me feel nauseous and excited at the same time. I saw things that made me feel desire and shock simultaneously. The audience reacted as if they knew what they were watching. They cheered at moments I didn't understand. Laughed at things that made my stomach tighten. Raised glasses like this was a celebration, not an unveiling. People spoke in different languages, but the reactions were the same, synchronized, instinctive. I felt like I had arrived late to a ceremony that everyone else had been attending for years. Every time I thought I had reached the edge of what was possible, the stage turned again. Something crazier happened; the previous moment suddenly looked tame, almost innocent. Limits

dissolved quietly, without announcement, until I realized I didn't know where the boundary had ever been. People stood up and left as if nothing had happened. New people took their seats within minutes, tickets exchanged, the ritual continuing uninterrupted. The show didn't acknowledge the change. It didn't pause. It didn't need an audience. It felt like it would keep going even if the room were completely empty. I stopped checking the time. I stopped reacting. I just watched. Like I was witnessing something that wasn't meant for daylight, something that existed only because it stayed hidden. I had the overwhelming sense that I had slipped behind the curtain of the world and seen the machinery turning. The danger wasn't in what I saw. It was in how quickly my mind adapted to it. How shock softened. How disbelief faded. How the impossible began to feel normal. I understood then that this wasn't about pleasure. It was about erasing edges. About removing context. About showing what happens when nothing is off-limits and no one looks away. I felt small. Uninvited. Like an observer who had wandered into a space meant only for believers. When I finally stood up, my legs didn't trust me. The exit felt too bright, too exposed. Outside, the street looked assembled incorrectly, like a stage set rebuilt from memory. That's when I saw her. She stood under a streetlamp, half inside the light, half outside it.

Layered fabrics draped her body, dark skirts brushing the cobblestones. Scarves were wrapped loosely around her shoulders and hair, patterned and worn, like they carried stories in the threads. Coins and metal hung from her neck and wrists, chiming softly when she shifted her weight. She didn't look dressed so much as assembled, intentional, symbolic, like she was playing a role older than the street itself. She watched me the way someone does when they already know the ending. "What did you see?" she asked. Not curious. Confirming. I told her. Not everything. Just enough. She nodded slowly, eyes never leaving mine, and smiled as if I'd passed some small, invisible test.

"You want to see something else?" she said. "Something most people never do."

I should have said no. Instead, I followed.

She led me away from the light, down a narrow street where the city noise collapsed behind us. My footsteps echoed against damp stone. We descended a short flight of stairs carved into the side of the canal. The water below was black and still, refusing reflection. The air grew colder here, heavier, as it pressed inward, like the ground itself was pulling us down.

At the end of the passage was a tunnel entrance set into the brick. A man waited there. He wore a long coat, a tall hat, and a cane resting lightly in his hand. His face was pale beneath darkened eyes, makeup carved into his features, making him look less alive and more ceremonial. Not threatening. Worse. Indifferent. Like a keeper of something that didn't require his belief, only his obedience. He said nothing. She told him a password, "silver-stream." He handed her a lantern. The light cut a thin, trembling circle into the darkness as she took it and stepped forward. I followed. The tunnel swallowed us immediately, damp and cold, sloping deeper with each step. Water dripped somewhere out of sight. The walls curved inward, close enough to feel breathless. With every step, the surface world peeled away quietly, without resistance, like it had never mattered. I felt like I was entering a different world. The tunnel opened into a cavern. It was vast. Far larger than it should have been. The ceiling disappeared into darkness. Bass rolled through the stone, low and constant, vibrating through my chest, through my bones. Light pulsed faintly through the mist hanging in the air. Water fell intermittently from above, not rain exactly, more like a deliberate cleansing, soaking bodies already in motion. They were everywhere. Naked bodies free from the burdens of the world. Not staged. Not performing. Moving. Masked faces turned without focusing. Painted skin glistened under shifting light. Costumes blurred fantasy and ritual, fabric clinging and separating as bodies passed through one another. Limbs intersected briefly, dissolved, reformed elsewhere. There was no center, no stage, no focal point. The space itself was the ceremony.

No one looked at me. That was worse than being watched. I stood at the edge, unnoticed, unnecessary. I wasn't invited forward. I wasn't turned away. That was the point. I realized then that this place wasn't about participation. It was about witnessing. About being allowed to see what happens when boundaries are removed, and no one flinches. When identity loosens. When the crowd becomes a single organism, breathing together, shifting together, consuming itself without urgency or shame.

The music never stopped. I walked into a smaller room. Stone beds everywhere. People intertwined in sexually intimate ways. I took off all my clothes and jumped in, like I was casually jumping into a pool made out of sex. There were so many people, I didn't know where I started, and everyone else began. People drifted in and out, as if on rotation. Faces changed. The movement didn't. Time stopped behaving like time. Minutes stretched. Hours collapsed. Shock softened into

familiarity. Disbelief dulled. The impossible began to feel routine, and that realization frightened me more than anything I was seeing. I felt myself disappearing. Not erased violently. Quietly. I felt small. Awake inside a dream that didn't care whether I understood it or not. When I finally climbed back through the tunnel, the lantern gone, the bass fading behind me, the sky above the canal was already lightening. Morning had arrived without permission. The city above looked wrong. Too clean. Too solid. Like a set rebuilt from memory.

I took a cab straight to the airport. My body moved without instruction. The night already felt unreal, like something my mind was trying to file away without language. As the plane lifted off, Amsterdam slipped beneath the clouds.

It didn't feel like I had visited a place.

It felt like I had passed through a layer of the world and come back carrying proof that it exists.

16

BANGKOK NEVER FORGETS

THERE WAS A NURSE I worked named Jasmine, who did not notice me at all. I noticed her immediately. She moved through the unit like an angel, Long black hair fell straight down her back, heavy and effortless, the kind that caught light without asking for it. She was petite and loud, with dark eyes. Her skin had a glow to it, not dramatic, just steady, like she carried good light with her wherever she went. I would not call it love. It was thinner than that and far more dangerous. Obsession without permission. Hope with nowhere to land.

Every time I saw her, I wanted one thing.

I wanted her to see me. She never did.

Months passed like that. Me noticing her.

Her passing by me. I existed in the same rooms as her without ever entering her awareness. Eventually, I came up with a plan that felt smooth in my head and humiliating in reality. I bought two Dutch Bros gift cards. Nothing grand. Just enough to say I thought of you without having to say it out loud. One day, I saw her giving report at the counter with another nurse.

I walked up behind them, heart pounding, hands sweating, rehearsed confidence evaporating with every step. I reached out to hand her one of the cards. Instead, I handed both of them to her friend. I did not realize what I had done until it was already over.

Her friend hesitated for a moment, confused, then casually handed one card to another nurse sitting nearby, who wasn't Jasmine. Just like that.

Months of planning collapsed in ten seconds. She never even touched one.

I walked away feeling stupid in a way that burned long after the moment passed.

Eventually, I asked her out anyway.

Somehow, she said yes. I floated for days afterward. I planned everything carefully.

A speakeasy downtown where you needed a password to get in. Dim lights. Dress nice.

Something intentional. After that, bumper cars. I had this idea that if she could laugh and crash into things and not take herself too seriously, she would be real. A keeper.

As if compatibility could be tested in a line for rides. A few days later, she canceled.

She said she was not in a position to date anyone. I believed her. And then I did not.

After that, every shift felt like punishment.

She stood with coworkers talking about men. Dates. Stories. Names that were not mine. Laughing easily, like the world was wide open to her. I learned how to disappear again. How to stand in the same space and take up none of it. A few months later, I tried one more time, just to fail again. I see it clearly now. I was not drawn to her. I was drawn to her damage. The familiar shape of it.

Childhood trauma. PTSD. That quiet ache I recognized immediately. I told myself the same lie I always told myself. If I love her enough, I can fix this. I can help. I can be the exception. I had done hypnotherapy before. It had helped me. So I bought her six sessions. Six hundred dollars.

It felt generous and purposeful. Like I was doing something good. Like healing could be a down payment on affection. She went once. It did not work for her. Not long after, she told me she was behind on rent. School had taken too much time. Work had slipped.

Panic lived just under her voice.

I got the refund from the hypnotherapy and handed her $500 in cash instead. No speech. No expectations.

Just help. And then she disappeared. Texts went unanswered. Plans dissolved. One night, I watched her Instagram story and saw a cabin. Steam rising from a hot spring.

A man's hand in the frame. Close. Casual.

Intimate. I stared at my phone longer than I wanted to admit. That was the moment something inside me collapsed.

Not anger. Not jealousy. Just that familiar recognition. I tried. I gave. I failed. Again.

After that, work became a hallway of ghosts.

We passed each other for months without speaking. I stared at the floor when she walked by. Pretended we had never shared anything. Pretended it had not mattered.

Like I had not built an entire future in my head that had never existed anywhere else.

I did not hate her. I hated how badly I wanted to be chosen. I hated how often I confused fixing with loving. I hated how easily hope turned into self-erasure.

She stayed beautiful the whole time.

I was the one unraveling.

The thing with Jasmine shouldn't have mattered.

Nothing happened.

No kiss.

No skin.

No moment you could point to and say, that's where it broke.

And somehow that made it worse.

I had tried so hard that my effort became the relationship. I built something in my head that never existed in real life. A version of her that smiled when I wasn't there. A future that only lived inside my chest. Wanting someone quietly, consistently, without ever being chosen back, does something to you. It doesn't explode. It erodes.

By the time I booked the ticket, I was already gone.

Bangkok felt far enough away to lose myself. By the time the plane touched down in Thailand, I was exhausted from thinking about someone who wasn't there. Bangkok hit me all at once. Heat that didn't care about you.

Air thick enough to chew.

Noise layered on top of noise until it stopped sounding like chaos and started sounding like a heartbeat.

I met Rudy at the airport.

Or at least, I met what used to be Rudy.

Fifteen years earlier, he was a party guy from Medford. Loud. Lean. Always chasing the next drink, the next night. I hadn't seen him since before life got heavy. Before consequences showed up.

The man rolling toward me wasn't who I expected.

He was bigger. Fifty pounds heavier at least. A white mullet that looked like it had given up halfway through its own existence. And then I noticed the wheelchair.

A security guard was pushing him.

No warning.

No explanation.

I stood there staring, trying to reconcile the version in my memory with the one in front

of me.

"What the fuck?" slipped out before I could stop it.

He laughed like it was nothing.

We exchanged the kind of hug you do when you're not sure where to put your arms anymore.

On the cab ride to the hotel, I converted four thousand dollars into Thai baht. The stack of bills was thick and absurd in my hands. For a moment, I felt rich in a way that

didn't make sense. Like money was suddenly a prop instead of a limit. Bangkok blurred past the windows. Street vendors still awake. Neon signs buzzing.

Motorbikes weaving between cars like rules were optional. Everything was alive.

At the hotel, reality snapped back.

I had booked my room properly. I knew we would land in the middle of the night. I planned for it.

Rudy hadn't.

They told him it would be fifty U.S. dollars to get into his room early.

He lost his mind.

"It's the principle," he said, voice already rising.

"It's fifty bucks," I said. "We're in Bangkok."

He refused. Decided to sit in the lobby for four hours instead. Arms crossed. Jaw tight.

Stubborn like it was a personality trait.

I didn't argue.

I went upstairs.

Hot water washed the airport off me. I stood there longer than I needed to, letting the

day dissolve down the drain. When I stepped out, it was 2 a.m.

Bangkok was just getting started.

I walked outside alone.

The city swallowed me immediately.

Clubs bleeding music into the street. Women calling out from doorways. Tuk-tuks idling like predators waiting for movement. Sweat. Perfume. Exhaust. Laughter that

sounded reckless instead of happy. Nana Plaza loomed ahead like a dare.

This was the part of Bangkok that people whispered about. Neon stacked three stories

high. Bars inside bars inside chaos. Desire was sold openly, shamelessly, like it was just

another commodity.

I had seen The Hangover 2. That was the extent of my preparation.

I stood there on the sidewalk, jet-lagged, heart pounding, cash thick in my pocket, the ghost of a girl from halfway across the world still lodged in my chest.

I thought to myself, almost amused,

What kind of trouble could I really get into?

Bangkok didn't answer.

It just opened its doors.

The moment I stepped outside, it stopped feeling real.

It wasn't just the street. It was everything. The parking lot. The sidewalks. The alleys.

The blocks stretching all the way toward Nana Plaza like a living corridor. Girls everywhere. Thousands of them. Lined up under neon signs, leaning out of doorways, pacing the curb, calling into the night.

I hadn't even taken ten steps before I felt it.

I stood out.

Six foot two. Two hundred and thirty pounds. American. Tattoos visible under the streetlights. I might as well have been wearing a spotlight.

They noticed instantly.

Hands reached for me as I passed. Sleeves tugged. Fingers brushed my arm, my chest, and my back. So many hands grabbing my junk every second, Voices stacked on top of each other, overlapping, urgent, practiced. "Hey."

"You."

"Handsome man."

"I go with you."

That phrase kept repeating. Over and over. Like a chant.

"I go with you."

Every few feet, someone else stepped into my path, smiling, touching, asking, promising. Not subtle. Not hesitant. It wasn't flirtation the way I knew it. It was transactional desire, blunt and relentless.

I kept walking, half stunned, half curious, making laps like I was trying to map the place in my head. The attention never stopped. It followed me down the street,

wrapped around me, pressed in from all sides.

I had never experienced anything like it.

Women had always liked me. That wasn't new. This was different. This wasn't being wanted. This was being hunted.

Nana Plaza rose ahead like a shrine built to excess.

Three levels high. Open-air. Bars stacked on bars. Music pouring out in waves. Inside were go-go bars, bright and loud, bodies moving under lights, dancers behind glass, on stages, in places designed to erase hesitation. It felt unreal, like the rules of normal life didn't apply here.

Outside, the street never slowed.

Nightclubs thumped. Vendors shouted. Neon flickered. And everywhere, tuk-tuks darted through traffic like insects, engines buzzing. Little three-wheeled taxis, half motorcycle, half cart, weaving through cars with no regard for lanes or mercy. They moved fast, loud, reckless, just like the city itself.

Eventually, I stopped resisting the pull of it. I locked eyes with one woman who wouldn't let go of my hand. She smiled like she already knew the answer. I didn't argue. I didn't think. I just nodded.

Back at the hotel, the system revealed itself.

A guard by the elevators took her ID. Calm. Routine. Like this happened a thousand times a night. Only then did we go up. Bangkok didn't trust anyone, but it knew how to manage risk.

Upstairs, everything moved fast and slow at the same time. A shower. Steam. Neon still flickering in my vision, even with the door closed. We slept together, and when it was over, she showered again, dressed without ceremony, and left like she'd never been there.

From downstairs, the phone rang.

The guard's voice was neutral. Professional.

"Everything okay?"

"Yeah," I said.

The line went dead.

It was barely three in the morning.

I stood there for a moment, alone in the room, the noise of the city still vibrating

through the walls. Then I showered again. Longer this time. Let the water run until the mirror fogged completely.

And then I went back out, gave in to another girl and did the exact same thing over again.

Same streets. Same lights. Same hands reaching. Same voices calling.

Only this time, something had shifted.

Jasmine was gone. The thought of her had slipped out somewhere between the crowd and the fire-lit

streets. Replaced by motion. Sensation. Noise. The kind of distraction that doesn't ask permission.

Bangkok didn't care who you were missing.

It just kept moving.

Jet lag hit us like a hangover we hadn't earned.

Rudy didn't want to move. He stayed in his room, curtains half-drawn, ordering food like the hallway was a border he couldn't cross. Every few hours, a knock came. A delivery. Sometimes, a woman from a dating site he'd found. They came and went

quietly. He didn't.

His body was betraying him in pieces. His feet swollen. His face flushed if he walked

too far. Sweat blooming instantly when he stood. There was something wrong with the

wiring, too. A delay between thought and action. He told me once, casually, about a

brain tumor, like it was weather. I didn't know what to say.

When we finally made it out for breakfast, the city was already in motion.

Bangkok doesn't wait for you to wake up.

We sat at a small restaurant, plastic chairs, a metal table, steam rising from plates that

came faster than we could order. Five courses for the price of a coffee back home.

Soup. Rice. Meat. Fruit. Something fried and perfect. Everything was sharp and alive with flavor.

The city moved around us like a current. Motorbikes threading through impossible gaps. Vendors shouting. People stepping into traffic without hesitation. If you didn't move with it, you got swallowed.

Later, we took a boat out on the river.

The river cut through the city like a spine. Brown water rolling heavy and calm, carrying everything. Old wooden houses on stilts leaned over the edge. Gold temples rose behind them, sharp and clean, catching the sun like they were built for it. Spires stacked with color and mirror, reflecting light back at the sky.

Monks passed by in orange robes. Tourists pointed. Locals didn't look twice.

Bangkok showed everything at once. Poverty. Reverence. Excess. History. No hierarchy. No apology.

Rudy complained the whole time.

About the price of the boat. About the guide. About the stops. He argued with strangers as if it were a sport. I kept paying just to keep us moving.

"Go with the flow," I told him.

He didn't hear it.

On the way back, a tuk-tuk driver smiled too wide.

"Cheap ride," he said.

I knew the script. The detour. The suit shop. The commission.

"No," I said. "Hotel."

He tried anyway. Turned the wheel. Slowed near a storefront.

I leaned forward.

"You take us home," I said, slow and clear. "Or I call the police."

His smile vanished.

A couple of locals glanced over. One nodded like he'd seen this movie before.

We went straight back.

Thailand was full of massage parlors. Everywhere. Neon signs. Open doors. Ten dollars an hour. No pretense. I went to one and lost track of time. Four hours disappeared under warm hands and quiet music. I went upstairs, slept, then went back down and did it again.

My first massage was with a mature, strong woman, her skin cracked by time.

She gave me the best massage of my life for an hour; I was in heaven. At the end, she turned me over, and before I knew what was happening, she started giving me what in America is called a "happy ending." I tried to stop her, and she immediately placed her hand over my lips and told me to shush. She wouldn't take no for an answer.

By nightfall, the city was ready.

The second night felt different.

I sat alone at a bar inside a go-go club. Music low. Lights soft. Someone placed a pitcher of beer in front of me. Open. I didn't think about it.

A woman touched my arm, tracing ink as if it were a map.

"Big tattooed man," she said, smiling. "You play pool?"

I shook my head.

She tried again. Scripted. Smooth. Predictable.

"No."

Another woman. Same words. Another after that. Same ending.

"Drink your beer."

I finished it.

When I stood up, the floor tilted.

Hard.

It felt like my body skipped ten steps ahead of my brain. Like gravity doubled without warning. I knew immediately. Too fast. Too sudden. I got outside before anything else could happen.

Bangkok blurred.

I sat down in a plastic chair outside a 7-Eleven. Neon buzzing. A homeless man sat beside me in his own chair, staring into nothing. Another thing Bangkok had

everywhere. 7-Elevens on every corner. Bright. Familiar. Safe.

I waited.

Let it pass.

Water. Time. Breathing.

Eventually, my body came back.

Upstairs, more water. Cold tile under my feet. My reflection unfamiliar but intact.

Later, when the city pulled me back out again, I went willingly.

Same streets. Same lights. Same hunger.

The night erased itself the only way it knew how.

Bangkok didn't judge.

It didn't care who you were running from.

It just kept going.

Thailand has its own rules.

It took me a couple of days to understand them.

There weren't just men and women. There was a third presence that existed openly,

confidently, without apology. Ladyboys. Everywhere. On the streets, in the bars, under the neon lights.

At first, I couldn't tell. But if you asked, they would tell you.

"I'm lady."

"I'm ladyboy."

No games. No trickery. Just truth, offered plainly.

One night, drunk and curious in that way travel makes you, I asked questions I'd never ask anywhere else. Numbers. Costs. Possibilities. They answered casually, like it was grocery math. A full transformation for less than what I'd spent on a few reckless weekends back home.

Every night blurred into the same ritual.

Thai beer. Heat. Nana Plaza glowing like a wound that refused to close. Hands reaching. Voices calling. The same words over and over.

"I go with you."

I let it happen.

Not because it felt good. Because it made everything else quieter.

For a week, I erased myself one night at a time. Faces blurred together. Rooms reset.

Mornings arrived without meaning. I stopped counting girls. I stopped caring. I wasn't chasing pleasure anymore. I was running from stillness.

Jasmine faded somewhere in the middle of it. Or maybe she didn't. Maybe I just buried her under repetition.

One night, a woman stood in the doorway of my room and looked around longer than the others had.

She smiled, not unkindly. "How many girls been here this week?" she asked.

I opened my mouth, then stopped.

"I don't know, I lost count," I said.

I wasn't lying. It was the truth.

She nodded like she understood something I didn't want to name.

When she left, the room felt bigger. Quieter. Like it was waiting for me to notice what

I'd been doing.

Bangkok never stopped offering doors.

I kept choosing the one that didn't make me think.

By then, Rudy barely left his room.

His body wouldn't cooperate. His feet swelled. Walking exhausted him. His thoughts

lagged behind his words like they were trying to catch up. So I stopped waiting for him. I went out alone.

Every night.

An American by himself, drifting through Bangkok until sunrise, learning which streets stayed loud, and which ones watched you back.

One night, I took a tuk-tuk across the city to Khao San Road.

It hit like a riot.

A hundred thousand people packed into one street. Bars spilling out onto the

pavement. Music clashing from every direction. Bodies pressed shoulder to shoulder,

moving without thinking. It felt like spring break had been stretched into a country. Vendors lined the edges, selling everything imaginable. Drinks. Trinkets. Bugs on

sticks. Fried scorpions. Tarantulas curled and blackened, legs stiff like wire.

I was drunk enough not to care.

I ate one.

The crowd roared like it mattered.

Nitrous balloons floated everywhere, bright and stupid, people sucking them down and laughing as if nothing existed beyond the next breath. The street pulsed. I let it carry me.

Then I saw a narrow path between buildings. Easy to miss. No sign. Just sound leaking out.

I followed it.

Underground, the bar was small and dark, walls sweating, speakers blasting pop punk. Blink-182 echoed off concrete. Thai kids jumped and shouted every word as if it were theirs. I stood there smiling, anonymous, watching something collide that shouldn't have worked but did.

It was perfect.

Later, I went back to Nana.

That's where I met Som.

She was small. Sharp smile. Beautiful looked like an Asian Playboy bunny. Confident without trying. I took her back to my room. And slept with her, the night always dissolved the same way all the others had.

The next day, she messaged me.

Lunch. Coffee. Normal things.

I ignored it. She kept trying. Asking to be my girlfriend like the word meant the same thing to both

of us. I didn't want one girlfriend. I wanted all of them.

Eventually, I gave in.

I went to see her at the bar where she danced. She sat on my lap like we'd known each other forever, brought me a drink, and laughed too loud. I drank it.

And then the floor tilted.

Again.

I knew the feeling now. The sudden drop. The way your body outruns your mind. I left before anything else could happen. I was roofied again.

Later, she found me furious, swearing she hadn't done anything to my drink. We argued. She cried. She apologized. So I took her to the room and slept with her again.

The next day, she wanted more. I disappeared. I found someone else. One night, I was standing in a 7-Eleven under harsh white lights, another girl beside me, when I felt it.

Being watched.

I turned.

Som stood there, eyes hard now, smile gone.

"So," she said quietly.

Looking furious. I ignored her and left with the girl.

The next night, she found me again. I gave in again and took her to my room.

Afterward, she asked me to go out for another drink.

I said no. Because this woman roofied me, and I knew it for a fact.

She left first. I followed not far behind. In the street, I saw her talking to a man on a

motorbike and kissing him. A large, insulated box strapped to the back of his bike, labeled "live organs," was sitting there. I caught a word I recognized. A phrase locals used when something didn't work.

"He didn't fall for it."

My stomach dropped.

Maybe it was nothing. Maybe it was paranoia. Or maybe Bangkok was finally showing me the edge of what I'd been flirting with all my life.

I didn't wait to find out.

That was my last night there.

The city didn't chase me. It didn't explain itself. It just kept going, loud and indifferent, offering the same doors to the next person who walked in, looking to disappear.

Bangkok ended without ceremony.

One morning, it was just over. No climax. No lesson. We boarded a bus and headed two hours south, away from the city and toward the coast.

Pattaya City.

When we arrived, it felt like we'd stepped into a different version of reality.

The air changed first. Salt instead of exhaust. Heat that wrapped instead of suffocated. The beach stretched wide and open, dotted with boats anchored just

offshore, hundreds of them bobbing gently like they'd been scattered there on purpose. Speedboats. Fishing boats. Tour boats painted bright colors, music pulsing

faintly across the water.

Paradise, if you didn't look too closely.

The beach was alive all day and all night. Thousands of people moving constantly.

Vendors shouting. Music drifting from every direction. The sun sat heavy in the sky, unapologetic. I spent hours walking barefoot along the sand, a mango smoothie sweating in my hand, watching everything without needing to be part of it.

People watching became its own kind of therapy.

I'd stop for a massage whenever I felt like it. No planning. No scarcity. Sometimes one. Sometimes four in a day. Time loosened. My body stopped keeping score.

But something else tightened.

By the time we got there, Rudy was becoming unbearable. Everything was a fight.

Every interaction a negotiation. I was exhausted from managing him. From slowing

myself down to match someone who couldn't move forward anymore. So I stopped.

I checked into a different hotel.

Didn't explain.

Didn't argue.

Didn't look back.

Week two of Thailand started alone.

That night, freshly showered, dressed, and slightly drunk, I wandered the streets with no destination. Pattaya glowed differently from Bangkok. Less chaotic. More deliberate.

Like the city knew exactly what it was offering.

That's when I saw him.

A big Black guy standing near the street, laughing, talking in English. The only English I'd heard in hours. I said something to him. I don't remember what. He grinned like

we'd known each other longer than five seconds.

"I gotta get your number," he said.

We exchanged WhatsApps. That's how everything worked there.

The next day, I messaged him.

He told me to meet him outside.

That's how I met Mangita.

He was solid. About my size, maybe bigger. About 260 pounds, muscle packed onto his frame like it belonged there. Thirty-seven. Calm. Confident. Looked like he'd

figured out how to exist anywhere.

When I found him, he was sitting outside eating pizza like nothing in the world was

urgent.

We talked. Laughed. Finished his food. Then he said, "Let's walk."

Soi 6 opened before us like a corridor designed to overwhelm.

A mile-long street. Bars lining both sides without interruption. And in front of every bar, women stood shoulder to shoulder, dressed promiscuously , waiting for prey. Thousands of them. Literally thousands.

Men walked down the center, as if they were being paraded.

The women shouted. Laughed. Grabbed. Pulled. Some carried inflatable hammers, beach toys, anything to touch you with. They swung them playfully, hit your legs, your arms, your chest. Hands everywhere. Voices calling out, begging, negotiating, competing.

"Pick me."

"Come here."

"I go with you."

It was relentless.

Mangita just laughed.

We walked the whole length of it, stunned, absorbing it as if it were unreal.

Eventually, without ceremony, we each chose. No romance. No buildup. Just selection.

We each picked a girl and went our separate ways.

Later, we went back out like it was again and did it again.

Past Soi 6 was Beach Road.

A long stretch running parallel to the water, lit by street lamps and neon. Women lined the sidewalk there too, standing in groups, alone, leaning against poles, walking beside you without asking. Same words. Same hands. Same pull.

Mangita and I walked that road up and down every day. No plans.

No clocks.

No consequences that felt immediate.

It was excess without friction. Desire without pretense. A week that felt detached from time entirely.

A week you couldn't forget even if you tried.

Pattaya didn't promise anything.

It just kept giving.

When I checked into my hotel, I saw a sign.

A simple symbol. The kind you'd see on a bathroom door back home. A man.

Stick-figure familiar.

And then a thick red X through it.

NO LADYBOYS.

I laughed out loud.

It was blunt. Unapologetic. So Thai it almost felt like a joke; they didn't care whether you understood or not. Rules posted in plain sight. No explanations offered.

Pattaya liked clarity.

Days disappeared there. We slept through the sun and woke with the heat already pressing against the windows. Nights belonged to the streets. So did Mangita and I.

Same rhythm, every day. Wake up late. Shower. Eat. Walk. Watch. Drift back into the noise once the sky went dark.

Walking Street was the heart of it.

A long stretch running straight toward the ocean, lit so bright it felt artificial. Clubs stacked shoulder to shoulder. Restaurants, shops, bars, and 7-Elevens squeezed between everything else. Performers filled the sidewalks. Fire dancers spinning flames. Music colliding from every direction. Somewhere above it all, fireworks cracked open the sky.

Out past the lights, the ocean reflected everything back. Massive casino boats floated offshore, glowing like cities detached from land.

The street never stopped moving.

Thousands of people walked it every night. Back and forth. No destination. Just motion. Girls everywhere, slipping into your path, catching your arm, smiling like they already knew how the night would end.

"I go with you."

Mangita moved through it like he belonged there.

He didn't drink. Didn't need to. The confidence I borrowed from alcohol lived in him naturally. We'd stop and talk to girls, and they'd ask where he was from.

He'd grin and say something outrageous.

"I'm from in your mouth."

They'd laugh like it was poetry.

Everything landed with him. Every word. Every look. He could say nothing and still be heard. I watched it happen over and over, impressed and slightly annoyed in the way you get when someone else makes something look effortless.

We went into clubs just to feel them. Massive rooms packed with bodies. A thousand people moving under strobes and bass. We didn't dance much. We watched. Took it in. Left when it stopped being interesting.

Some girls asked for his number. He gave it without thinking. No weight attached. I never asked if he called her.

Not everyone wanted us.

Some women waved him off with a smile that wasn't friendly. "No," they said. "You, Chocolate Man."

They laughed when they said it. Like it was a joke they'd practiced.

"Chocolate Man hurt me last time."

Others ignored me entirely.

"White Boy," one said dismissively, already turning away. They preferred Indian guys.

Arab guys. The rules shifted depending on who was standing in front of them.

Pattaya didn't pretend otherwise.

We wandered into a Russian bar by accident.

It felt different the moment we sat down. Darker. Tighter. Drinks overpriced. Tips expected, not suggested. The girls moved with rehearsed precision, eyes scanning constantly.

One of them leaned in close to me.

"Come to my room," she said softly.

Everything in my body said no.

I glanced toward the back and caught a glimpse through a half-open door. A man sitting at a table, heavyset, expressionless. He slid bullets into a magazine slowly, counting them, money stacked beside his hand.

I didn't need more information.

I stood up immediately. Paid. Left. Didn't look back.

Some places don't warn you. They just let your instincts decide.

We finished the night the same way we finished most of them. Walking Beach Road.

The ocean on one side. Streetlights stretching endlessly ahead. Women lining the sidewalks, standing alone or in pairs, calling out, stepping closer, touching your arms as you passed.

"I go with you."

By then, the words barely registered. They were part of the landscape.

Eventually, Mangita nodded toward one girl. I nodded toward another. No discussion.

No ritual. Just separation.

That was Pattaya.

Every night folded into the next. Pleasure without memory. Risk without consequence that felt immediate. The city didn't hide what it was offering, and it didn't care what you did with it.

It just stayed lit, stayed open, and waited for you to decide how far you were willing to go.

When it was over, it was like leaving a dream.

17
FALLING APART

THE CALL CAME THE way those calls always do. Quiet. Ordinary. Like the world was not about to end. Mitchell had pancreatic cancer. There are some words you hear once, and your body understands them before your brain does. Pancreatic was one of those words. Mitchell was my godfather.

But that word never felt big enough. He was my rock. The one who stayed. The one who answered. The one who filled the empty spaces left behind by everyone else.

He was the only real father figure I had as an adult. The only family I had left that felt solid. When I found out, I stopped functioning. I missed work. I stayed in bed. I stared at the walls. Grief did not come in waves. It came like gravity, pulling everything down with it. I did not bounce back. I did not regroup. I just sank.

Around that time, I found my biological father, John. We started talking constantly. Every day. Long conversations. Real ones. He told me about his health. He had an aneurysm in his chest. The widow-maker.

He brushed it off. Told me not to worry. Told me he was fine. I wanted to believe him.

My kids talked to him. They laughed with him. We planned a trip to Arizona. I let myself imagine something I had never had. A future where he stayed alive long enough to matter.

A few months later, John dropped dead.

The aneurysm took him. No warning. No goodbye. Just gone.

The last family I had left disappeared right after I found him.

That loss did not just hurt. It hollowed me out.

I did not recover. I could not.

I went back to work because that is what you are supposed to do. But my mind was not there anymore. I worked in a hospital surrounded by emergencies while my own nervous system stayed stuck on high alert. I could not focus. My chest hurt constantly. Anxiety lived in my body like a second heartbeat. Pain stacked on pain until it felt endless.

My manager had recently taken over the department. She was like a sister to me. Someone I trusted. She made changes. Big ones. And I could not keep up. Not because I did not care. Because I was drowning.

One day, it all collapsed.

I had a panic attack at work so bad that they sent me home.

When I got there, the police were waiting.

Two officers stood in the open. Two more were hidden behind bushes with their hands on their guns. I felt surrounded. Like I had already done something wrong.

Like they were preparing to take me away.

They thought I was going to kill myself.

I stood on my own front lawn and had to convince a stranger with a badge and a gun that I wanted to live. Thirty minutes of explaining. Of pleading. Of trying to sound stable while my insides were on fire.

I told them the truth. I have kids. I would never leave them.

But fear does not care about truth. It only listens to optics.

That night broke something in me. Not because of the police. Because I realized how bad it had gotten without me noticing.

I left that job soon after. A career of six years. Gone.

I walked away and started over because I no longer recognized myself.

Shortly after, I had been dealing with really bad neck pain from the football accident, so I got an MRI. Just to be safe. They found an aneurysm in my brain.

I thought about John. About how fast he went. About how fragile everything suddenly felt.

Not long after that, he was gone.

And that was it, now one lived in me.

I broke in a way that made 2015 look gentle by comparison. I did not just fall apart. I disappeared. I clawed my way through days without recognizing myself. I survived something I do not fully remember surviving.

I was desperate. On the edge.

Then I got the call that rocked my entire world.

Mitchell was dead. I remember when I got the call. Sitting there frozen, staring at a wall for 12 hours.

He faded in pieces, slowly enough that everyone learned how to pretend it was not happening yet. His voice softened first. Then his posture. Then the way time seemed to move around him was different, like the world had already started letting him go while he was still standing in it.

I could feel it coming months before the call ever came. I felt it at work, when my chest tightened for no reason. I felt it at night, when sleep would not stay. I felt it every time I braced myself for news I did not want but somehow already knew.

Mitchell was never loud about what he did for me. He did not announce himself as a savior. He just showed up. Again and again. When my parents died, and the ground dropped out from under me, he did not let me fall alone. He stepped into the empty space without asking for credit. Without asking for thanks. He became the structure.

He taught me how to stand when no one else was there to hold me up. He helped me fight for guardianship. He taught me how to raise my brothers when I was still barely surviving myself. He showed me how to be an adult when I was still a kid.

He did not fix everything. He just stayed. And that mattered more.

Every birthday, without fail, there was something. A gift. A call. A reminder that I was still seen. Still worth remembering. Even when the rest of the world felt like it had moved on.

So when his health started slipping, my body knew before my mind would accept it. I tried to prepare. I told myself I was ready. I told myself grief could be rationed if you anticipated it early enough. That if I cried a little each day, it would not destroy me all at once.

That was a lie.

The call came anyway. Ordinary. Unceremonious. A voice on the other end saying words that did not fit the shape of the moment. He is gone.

And something inside me collapsed.

I cried the way people cry when they are not just losing a person, but an entire era of their life. The way you cry when the last adult who knew your whole story leaves with it. When the final witness to who I was before the damage is suddenly gone.

At the funeral, I listened to people talk about how much Mitchell meant to them. I heard stories I had never heard before. Pieces of him I had not known. And then I stood up and spoke too.

I do not remember what I said.

I remember the tears. I remember the microphone shaking. I remember the room going quiet in a way that felt heavy and sacred at the same time.

After everyone left, I stayed. Twenty minutes. Maybe longer. Just standing there, looking at him, unable to leave. Like if I stayed still enough, time might rewind. Like maybe the world would realize it made a mistake.

Later, when I held his hand one last time, the weight of it hit me fully. This was the last time I would ever touch the man who stepped in when my parents could not. The last physical proof that I had not imagined any of it. That the love was real. That the safety was real.

Grief did not come as chaos. It came as silence. The kind that sits next to you. The kind that does not scream. The kind that just stays.

Mitchell did not just leave a hole. He left a responsibility. To live in a way that honors the man who refused to abandon me. To keep going, even when everything in me wanted to stop. To be for others what he was for me, even when it hurts.

I lost my last family member that day. But I did not lose what he gave me. That stays.

And someday, when the pain softens enough to breathe again, I realized something quietly devastating and beautiful at the same time.

Mitchell did not save me so I could survive.

He saved me so I could live. And he still does.

A year after Mitchell was gone, the mail came like it always did.

Bills. Ads. Things that needed attention.

And then there was a package that did not make sense.

It was not large. It was not heavy. Just ordinary brown cardboard, taped cleanly, my name on the label. No explanation. No note. Just something forwarded from an estate that had already said goodbye.

Inside was a Bible.

Worn. Soft at the edges. The kind that had been opened and closed enough times to remember hands. The kind you do not buy for decoration. The kind you live with.

When I opened the cover, my name was engraved inside. Not scribbled. Not rushed. Carefully. Intentionally. Like it had always known where it was going.

I sat there longer than I needed to, holding it, letting the weight of it settle. A year late. Perfectly timed. A message that had crossed distance and death without asking permission.

It felt like him.

Not dramatic. Not loud. Just there when I needed it most.

I imagined him planning it. Somewhere in the quiet before the end, thinking ahead. Making sure I would not be left empty-handed again. Making sure I would have proof that even gone, he was still watching the door.

It was not about religion. It was about reassurance. About a man who stepped in when my parents could not. Who carried us when we were breaking. Who stayed steady when everything else shook. A man who never needed recognition, only follows through.

The Bible did not feel like a goodbye. It felt like a hand on my shoulder. Like him saying what he had always said without words.

I have got you.

And for the first time since he died, I believed it again.

Mitchell did not leave me nothing. He left me a life that held. A spine strong enough to keep standing. A quiet voice that still answers when I need it.

Some people save you in emergencies. Others save you across time.

He was the second kind.

And I carry him with me.

Still.

18

A CAT DANCING ON MY GRAVE

I DIDN'T SEE HER at first.

That's how it always happens. Noise everywhere. Comments piling up under my posts, names and faces blurring together. Attention is cheap when it comes in waves. She was there for a while. Watching. Liking. Commenting quietly while I wasn't paying attention. When I finally noticed her, it felt like a switch flipped. I didn't ease into it. I never do. Once she was in my sight, everything else dimmed. We started talking constantly. Long conversations that stretched late into the night. Messages that didn't feel like small talk, more like confessions. The first real thing she ever told me wasn't soft. "I'm psycho," she said. "I don't know which of my six personalities you're talking to today." I laughed because that's what people do when they don't want to hear the warning embedded in the sentence. I thought she was exaggerating. Being edgy. Being funny. She wasn't.

Lucy was about five-four, maybe a hundred and fifteen pounds, and built with an almost unreal precision, like God didn't create her; he took his time with her. Pale skin that never tanned, the kind that caught light instead of absorbing it, like porcelain that somehow stayed warm. She spent hours in the gym, and it showed in the quiet certainty of her body. Perfect legs. Long, clean lines. A balance that made her movements feel intentional even when she was doing nothing at all. Her breasts were large, perfect in the way you don't question. My body would recognize them way before my mind ever did. Everything about her felt calibrated, like she existed exactly the way she was supposed to, exactly what I had always dreamed of. She had black hair that framed her face perfectly. Big black glasses because she couldn't see without them, which only made her more adorable. There was something about the contrast, the sharpness of her body, paired with that vulnerability. When she looked at you through those lenses, it felt like being chosen. She reminded me of a Kardashian-type at first glance, polished, striking, and undeniable, but that comparison fell apart the longer I knew her. Kardashians feel designed. Lucy felt discovered. Like something rare you spent your whole life searching for. Something you weren't supposed to find and somehow did anyway. Every time I saw her, I fell in love with her again and again. Not metaphorically. Literally. The feeling stacked. Layered. Built on itself until it became gravity. I didn't admire her from a distance. I orbited her. I measured rooms by whether or not she was in them. When she walked toward me, everything else blurred. When she touched me, it felt like confirmation. She was everything I had ever wanted. A pale angel with sharp edges. Beautiful without effort. Powerful without cruelty. Fragile in ways she never announced. Looking at her felt like standing too close to something holy, but at the same time, something on fire. Like if I stared long enough, I might ruin it just by wanting it too much. Trying to see her in person was chaos from the start. We made plans over and over again. Always her idea. Always her excitement. "Let's cuddle," and then she just wouldn't show up. Ten times at least. No explanation. No apology. Sometimes she'd vanish completely. Once, she deleted me without a word when we had plans, and I asked where she was. I remember staring at my phone, trying to reverse-engineer what I had done wrong, coming up empty every time. And then she'd reappear as if nothing had happened. When we finally did get together offline, it felt explosive. Immediate. Like two people crashing into something they'd been circling for a long time. We blurred lines fast. Too fast.

One night, in the middle of sex, when she was on top of me, I asked her to be my girlfriend. It didn't feel crazy in the moment. It felt like fate. She said yes. We lasted a day. The fight that ended it that time started over something so small it should've meant nothing. A TV show. A character, she asked me if I thought she was hot. I answered honestly. She erupted. Accusations, jealousy, and anger that didn't match the moment. She left, and I stood there confused, already feeling the pattern forming. That was the relationship. On and off. Together and gone. Love followed immediately by disappearance. Every time we reconnected, it felt deeper. Every time she left, it hurt worse. I fell in love with her in a way that scared me. The kind where you imagine a future without needing to say it out loud. She talked about marriage. About kids. About wanting a life that felt safe and real. And I wanted that too. I wanted it with her. I wanted to build something steady out of all the chaos we both carried. She had told me why she was the way she was. Her long-term boyfriend had overdosed and died. A sudden, brutal loss that fractured her ability to trust permanence. Love, to her, was something that disappeared without warning. Anyone who got close risked becoming another ghost. She didn't know how to let someone love her without waiting for the moment it all collapsed. Knowing that didn't make it easier. It made me try harder. I carried her to bed to put her to sleep. Undressed her carefully. Tucked her in. Kissed her forehead. She trusted me to do things sexually that she had never done before. Those moments felt sacred, like I was protecting something fragile that the world had already taken too much from. I thought if I loved her gently enough, consistently enough, she might believe it wouldn't vanish. But the volatility never stopped. Four to six months of emotional whiplash. And then I tried to anchor us to something solid. Every time she disappeared, my nervous system would spiral out of control. I felt like I was withdrawing from drugs. She was my heroin, my trauma bond. Disneyland. I bought us the tickets. All of them. Spent thousands. It felt symbolic. A memory. A reset. Something joyful we could hold onto. We fought again, broke up again, so I changed her ticket to my son's name. Then we made up again. It was supposed to be the three of us going. The night before the trip, my other son called me crying. He wanted to go too, so I bought him tickets as well. When I told her, she shut down. " If this is going to turn into some kids' trip," she said. "I'm not going, I'm not going to have fun." So I went without her. I posted everything. Every ride. Every smile. Every moment. Because every time she watched my stories, it felt like she was there. Like I was sharing the experience with her anyway. She watched every single one.

I remember making the long drive to LA. I constantly pictured her tiny, perfect little body sitting in the passenger seat next to me. Wishing, hoping she was there. But she wasn't. When I got back, a week later, it was her birthday. I bought her a Lady Gaga record. Wrote her a sweet birthday card. Told her how deeply I loved her. We had sex all over my house. Couch, bed, shower, for hours and hours. I had never felt closer to another person in my life. It felt like maybe this time, things would finally stabilize. Maybe this time she would stay. She didn't. She started disappearing again. Days at a time. No responses. No explanations. Then she'd come back as if nothing had happened. And every disappearance ripped something open in me. Old abandonment wounds I thought I had outgrown. Fear that sat in my chest and refused to move. She had told me she struggled with suicidal ideations before. So every silence felt dangerous.

Every unanswered message felt like something terrible waiting just out of reach. I was worried constantly. Helpless. Watching someone I loved unravel while being completely shut out. Her life collapsed in every possible way. She lost her job. Her car was repossessed. She caught charges with the law. She was losing me, too, or maybe choosing to. I couldn't tell. When her car was impounded, she asked me for money. A couple of hundred dollars. I drove to the house to give it to her. When she came outside, she looked at me like she didn't know me. Like a stranger, like none of it even happened. She gave me an awkward hug. No warmth. No recognition. I handed her the money. Then that was it; I watched her walk away. That was the last real moment we had. After that, she ignored me completely. Something inside me broke, and I lost my mind. Not just because of her. Because it stacked on top of everything else. Losing my career after six years. Losing her. Getting diagnosed with a brain aneurysm. Losing Mitchell. Losing my biological father. All of it collapsed inward at once. It felt like 2015 all over again, except this time I was ten years older and somehow even less equipped to survive it. I lost my mind. If Randy hadn't been there, I don't know if I would still be alive today. He talked to me every night for six months. Literally. Phone calls that lasted until the early morning. He listened while I spiraled, while I tethered of the edge of life and death. While I repeated myself. While I couldn't see a way out. He didn't try to fix me. He just stayed. He listened. Over and over again, he kept me alive. And the cruelest part was this. She kept watching. Every story I posted, she was there. One of the first views. Silent. Always silent. I sent her voice messages. Long ones. Apologies. Confessions. Love. Five-minute recordings sent over and over again into nothing. She never responded. She just watched. For months. And it destroyed me. As she kept watching me, my mind started filling in the blanks on its own.

Every morning, that was the first thing I checked. Not messages. Not notifications. Her. I would watch her watching me. And the moment I saw her face appear in that small circle on Instagram, something inside me loosened. She's still here. She's still watching. I still have a chance. That was enough to keep me going. So I started building stories on my Instagram for her. Carefully. Obsessively. Everything I posted was aimed in her direction. Every song choice. Every caption. Every photo. Sometimes I tried to look strong. Sometimes broken. Sometimes indifferent. Sometimes nostalgic. I was throwing signals into the dark, hoping one of them would land. I did it all for her. For months, my life existed through that lens. If she watched, I felt alive. If she didn't, I felt like I was disappearing. That little circle became proof that I hadn't been erased yet. I held onto that illusion for almost three months. And during those three months, I was falling apart. I was in the worst shape of my life. Depressed in a way that wasn't just sadness, but physical.

My nervous system felt permanently switched on. Panic attacks hit me at work without warning. My chest would tighten. My heart would race. My body felt like it was burning from the inside out. All day, every day, anxiety sat in my bones. I couldn't focus. I couldn't think straight. Sometimes I would drift so far out of myself that nothing felt real. I'd be walking, talking, driving, but it felt like I was watching my life from a distance. Like someone else was steering and I was just a passenger, trapped behind my own eyes. Dissociation is the only word I've found for it. And it was terrifying. Something broke in my head during that time. I still don't fully understand it. I just know that the person I was before those months didn't come out the same on the other side. Every day got worse. Then worse again. I reached a point where I couldn't imagine continuing like that. I called a friend in a panic, unraveling, telling her I didn't know how much longer I could live inside that pain. That I was desperate for relief from a nervous system that wouldn't shut off, from a mind that wouldn't stop replaying the same question. How could someone I loved that deeply care so little? She wouldn't talk to me. Wouldn't call. Wouldn't give me closure. Nothing. Just silence. And watching. It felt like losing her reopened every loss I'd ever survived. Like my parents. Like Mitchell. Like every person I had loved and buried. It was as if they all disappeared again at the same time, collapsing into one unbearable weight. But the worst part was that she was still alive. I was at the edge of myself. Then my friend called. Her voice cut through the noise. "Come to the mountain," she said. I listened.

19

AYAHUASCA SHADOWS

Before Lucy disappeared completely, there was a letter. Not a text. Not a message. Not something typed and deleted a hundred times. A real letter. Handwritten. Pages long. The kind of thing you don't write unless you mean every word. I had written it for her weeks earlier, a couple of weeks after her birthday, pouring everything into it. How much I loved her. How deeply. How serious I was. How I wasn't playing. How I wanted a life with her. Marriage. Kids. All of it. No games. No irony. Just truth. I planned to give it to her the day I brought her the money for her car. But when she stepped outside, when she looked at me like I was already gone, I froze. I could feel it in my chest. The timing was wrong. The moment was wrong. I was afraid that handing it to her then would only make things worse. So I didn't. I kept it in my pocket. When I got home, I put the letter back on my dresser. It stayed there for months. Every morning, I saw it. Every night, I passed it. A quiet promise waiting for a moment that never came. I kept thinking there would be another chance. Another conversation. Another version of us where it would finally matter. There was a key too. I had bought it earlier, before everything fractured. It was a small key, with Minnie Mouse on it. A stupid detail. A perfect one. Disneyland. Us. The trip that was supposed to mean something that didn't happen. The key wasn't symbolic to me. It was literal. It meant she had somewhere to come back to. That she wasn't floating. That she had a home. With me. She never got the letter. She never got the key. On the way to the retreat, I stopped at Harris Beach. Brookings, Oregon. It was raining. Not softly. The kind of rain that soaks through everything. Fog pressed low against the shoreline, swallowing the horizon. The ocean was violent. Waves crashing hard against the rocks, exploding into white foam before being dragged back out again. It looked exactly how I felt. I walked the beach alone, collar pulled up, shoes filling with sand. I had the letter folded in my hand. The key in my pocket. I watched the water over and over, each wave arriving with force, leaving nothing behind. I sat down on a rock near the edge of the shore. The wind cut through me. The rain stung my face. I stared at the water and imagined her reading the letter. Imagined her understanding. Imagined it finally landing. All the things I had never been able to say out loud. I took the letter and rolled it carefully. I found an empty Absolut vodka bottle. Slid the letter inside. Dropped the key in after it. Glass clinked softly. I stood up, walked closer to the edge, and held the bottle in both hands. The ocean roared in front of me. Endless. Indifferent. Immense. I held the glass in my hands for a good minute, and just thought to myself, if she only knew. If she only knew my love ran this deep. If she only knew it wasn't casual. If she only knew I would have given her everything. I threw the bottle as hard as I could. It disappeared into the waves immediately. No ceremony. No pause. Just gone. I filmed it. Posted it. She watched. And still said nothing. No message. No reaction. No acknowledgment. The ocean took the letter. She took the silence. And in that moment, standing alone on the beach, soaked and shaking, I understood something I had been refusing to accept. None of it mattered to her. Not the letter. Not the key. Not the love. I didn't matter.

I drove until the road stopped feeling real. Past towns that barely registered as places. Past gas stations that looked like they'd been waiting years for a car. Then to a small hippy town called Garberville, California, somewhere I had never even heard of. I drove up a dirt road higher and higher. One hour up a mountain, the kind of climb where your ears pop, and your phone goes dead without service at the same time. No way to be reached, even if someone wanted to find you. It was intentional. At the top, the road opened into something that didn't make sense at first. Cabins tucked into trees. A recreation hall that looked like it had been built to host secrets. Fire pits arranged like gathering points, not decoration. With a huge circular temple in the middle of it. Everything was clean. Thoughtful. Expensive in a way that didn't need to advertise itself. It felt like the edge of the world. Like a hidden chapter no one talked about. Like a place that only existed if you were already lost enough to find it. This wasn't a campground. It was a retreat. The kind of place rich people disappear to when money stops working. The kind of place you don't stumble into by accident. Everyone there had paid nearly five thousand dollars to be there. Five thousand dollars for a guided journey led by shamans flown in from Brazil. Real ones from a village in the rainforest. Not Instagram wellness influencers. Men and women who carried themselves like they'd seen things most people spend their lives running from. I didn't belong there on paper. A friend pulled strings. Got me in for almost nothing. Everyone else arrived in luxury SUVs, helicopters, private jets, designer luggage, quiet confidence built on money and desperation. CEOs. Tech people. Artists. Heirs. Hippies with trust funds. People who looked successful on the outside and were wrecked underneath. Broken people who had finally run out of ways to distract themselves. There was no small talk. No introductions that mattered. You could feel it immediately. Everyone was there for the same reason, even if no one said it out loud. They were trying to heal something they couldn't outrun anymore. The air felt different. Thinner. Charged. Like whatever you brought with you up that mountain wasn't going back down intact. And standing there, surrounded by strangers who had paid obscene amounts of money to feel human again, I realized something quietly terrifying. This wasn't an escape. It was a confrontation of pain. And I had driven one hour past the last signal on purpose. Ayahuasca: Night One. I walked into the temple and immediately felt how small I was. About one hundred people were already inside. Small mattresses were laid out in a wide circle of the temple, each one with a bucket placed carefully at the foot. Everything felt deliberate. Prepared. Like everyone else had already accepted what was about to happen. Several shamans entered. Colorful ceremonial robes, with matching headdresses, and full makeup. They spoke calmly about the medicine. About how it could reach places therapy never could. How one night on the medicine is stronger than ten years of therapy. About how pain hides in the body when it is carried long enough, and the medicine seeps it out. They didn't promise comfort. They promised truth. They handed me a shot glass. The liquid inside was brown and dull. I swallowed it. It tasted like fire and earth. Bitter. Heavy. It burned all the way down. I waited. Nothing happened. An hour passed. My mind stayed sharp. My body stayed quiet. I took another. Then another. Three total. Still nothing. I wondered if something was wrong with me. If I was too numb for this to work. Then the shaman began walking the circle. He sang in his native tongue. The sound didn't feel like music. It felt ancient. The ceiling began to breathe. I saw it. The walls expanded and contracted with the rhythm of his voice. I felt the medicine finally arrive, not in my head, but straight into my chest. It felt like my heart was being hugged. Around me, people were vomiting. Crying. Breaking open. I stayed still. I saw everything. The chanting grew louder. Not louder in volume, but heavier, like it had weight. The drumbeat slowed until it felt synchronized with my pulse. The air inside the structure thickened, colors bending at the edges, firelight stretching and collapsing like it couldn't decide what shape it wanted to be. That's when I looked up. The doorway was framed in wood darkened by age and smoke, a threshold that felt older than the mountain itself. The shaman stood near it, singing in a language I didn't understand, his voice cutting through the space like it was opening something instead of filling it. And then I saw her. Lucy stood in the doorway. But not the Lucy I knew. She was smaller. Thinner. Dim, like the light refused to land on her fully. It was her face, unmistakable, but younger. Childlike. As if time had been peeled back and left only the version of her that had learned how to survive instead of how to stay. She didn't step inside. She didn't move forward. She just stood there, half in shadow, half erased. For a moment, I thought it was my mind filling in a memory. Grief playing tricks. But then she looked directly at me. Locked eyes. And I felt it in my chest, sharp and immediate, like something had found its mark. Her mouth moved. No sound came out at first. She kept trying. Lips forming shapes that didn't land anywhere. Like the words were stuck behind glass. Her face tightened with effort, frustration, and desperation. She was trying to say something that had been waiting too long. Then, finally, silently, clearly, I understood her. I'm sorry. Her mouth shaped it slowly. I'm sorry. Her eyes changed when she said it. Not relief. Not peace. Just the raw exhaustion of someone who had carried something too heavy for too long. Then the second sentence came. I didn't know how to love you. The moment those words finished forming, the air around her shifted. Darkness gathered behind her, not like smoke drifting, but like it had intent. It poured in from the edges of the doorway, thick and fast, swallowing the light around her shoulders, her arms, her hair. She didn't fight it. She didn't run. She looked at me one last time. Her eyes were watering with tears. And then it took her. Not gently. Violently. The blackness wrapped around her like hands and yanked her backward with impossible speed. One second she was there, the next she was gone, ripped out of the doorway so fast it felt like reality snapped shut behind her. The doorway was empty. The chanting never stopped. The door slammed shut. The fire kept flickering as if nothing had happened. But I was shaking. My chest burned. My hands felt hollow. Whatever I had just seen didn't feel symbolic in the moment. It felt like something had been removed. Like a chapter had been torn out instead of closed. I sat there, breathing, trying to convince myself I was still in my body, still on the mountain, still surrounded by strangers chasing healing. I felt everything in ways I didn't know were possible. Suddenly, I was somewhere else. I was the big old house. Kevin and Micky were alive. They stood on the porch smiling, dancing to the music the shaman was playing. They looked whole. Untouched by sickness. Untouched by time. Kevin laughed the way I remembered, standing up straight without pain. Micky's eyes were bright, warm, and familiar. They told me it was okay. That everything had always been okay. They told me they never left. They asked me if I could feel it. I screamed yes. Because I could. For the first time. The music changed. Drums. Guitar. Strong. Alive. Vibrant. The sound felt like the person I had always wanted to be. With every beat, I felt stronger. More present. More real. I saw a heart covered in pain, coated in thick black sludge. I knew immediately it was mine. Without hesitation, I reached into my chest, scooped the blackness out, and threw it away. My heart started beating as it had never beaten before. I felt like I belonged somewhere. Like I mattered. I felt a deep love I had never felt in my life. It was me loving myself like I'd never known how. It had been there the entire time. I just never knew how to reach it. Ayahuasca: Night Two. At 9:30 p.m., I walked back down to the temple. The crowd was lively. Cheerful. Open. Strangers came up to me and asked about my pain like it was normal. And when I told them, they didn't flinch. They listened. They hugged me. They stayed. I felt supported in a way I never had before. At 11 p.m., I took one drink of the medicine. Nothing happened. I lay there for two hours staring at the ceiling, waiting. My mind stayed intact. My body stayed quiet. I wondered if the night before had been a fluke. At 1 a.m., I took another. Still nothing. Shortly after, a third. That's when everything collapsed. Everything I had been running from for years came rushing through me all at once. Not as thoughts, but as sensation. It surged through my body like electricity. My chest tightened. My limbs vibrated. The air felt too loud. Too close. I stood up and vomited harder than I ever had in my life. My body purged like it was trying to survive something toxic. I puked in the bucket at my feet. Years of trauma escaped me. The room began to spin. The shaman. The music. The people. The walls. Everything collapsed into one overwhelming wave. I was certain I was dying. I had to leave. I stumbled into the lobby and sat on a bench, barely holding myself upright. I almost fell backward and cracked my head open on the floor. I remember thinking, This is it. Goodbye world. Goodbye to my kids. Goodbye everyone. I couldn't do this. And yet I went back inside. I barely made it to my mat before I collapsed. My body was still shaking. My thoughts were fragmented, splintered into noise and fear. I could feel something dark clinging to me, heavy and sticky, like it didn't want to let go. The shamans saw it immediately. All of them surrounded me without asking, moving with a calm that felt ancient, practiced. Hands pressed gently against my shoulders, my chest, my back. Someone rubbed a thick lotion into my skin, sharp and citrusy, all over my body. It was like lemon and smoke, while another fanned feathers slowly across my entire body. Back and forth. Over my arms. Across my chest. Down my spine. I could see it happening. Not metaphorically. Visually. Darkness lifting off me in strands. Pulling away like smoke being dragged upward. Leaving my body in pieces. Every pass of the feathers made my breathing slow just a little more. Every touch grounded me further back into myself. I wasn't fighting anymore. I was being emptied. When it finally passed, when my body stopped resisting, I collapsed back onto the mat like I had run out of strength entirely. I laid there for what felt like forever. It was one of the worst experiences of my life. The pain was unbearable. What I had been carrying all these years felt like death itself. I felt every second of it. I was trapped in my own personal hell with no exit. Then something shifted. I came out of it slowly and realized I wasn't dying. My ego was. And it needed to. For hours afterward, I curled into myself and cried harder than I ever had. I cried like something dark was being pulled out of me. When I looked up, I saw heaven. I saw Kevin and Micky again. I saw God removing the pain from my chest piece by piece. After the last piece was gone, I heard his voice clearly. I love you, son. I never left you. I felt light. Full. Calm. Happy. For the first time in as long as I could remember, my mind was quiet. That's when I felt a hand take mine. She was sitting beside me the entire time. I didn't know how I hadn't noticed her before. She didn't speak. She didn't ask permission. She just held my hand like she understood exactly how bad it had been. Like she knew words would only get in the way. Her energy moved into my hand immediately. Warm. Steady.

And I felt mine move into hers at the same time. A quiet exchange. Back and forth. That connection was the only thing that kept me anchored. Every time my mind started to drift again, I focused on her hand. The pressure. The warmth. The reminder that I wasn't alone. She stayed with me for hours. She held me. Not sexually. Not possessively. Just... there. Her body curved around mine, protective, grounding. I hadn't been held like that since Lucy. The familiarity startled me. The difference did too. It felt the same in my body, but different in my chest. Less sharp. Less desperate. She had red hair, vivid even in the low light. An athletic body, sculpted and strong. The kind of beauty that would stop people cold in the outside world. The kind most men would chase without hesitation. But in that space, stripped of performance, she felt softer than she looked. Present. Human. When the ceremony finally ended, she walked me back to my cabin without a word. At the door, she hesitated, then quietly asked if she could stay. Not with expectation. Just... stay. What happened after didn't feel frantic or consuming. It felt slow. Connected. Like something unfolding instead of being taken. We spent the night together, and then the day after, moving in and out of each other without urgency. Then six hours of nonstop sex. It felt like everything I needed to feel ok again. Without fear. It felt like bonding, not escape. Like a shared landing after free fall. And still, even in that beauty, I could feel the pattern watching from a distance. The timing. The intensity. The way the connection arrived only after the collapse. Different woman. Different ceremony. Same part of me reaching out to be held, but not knowing how to hold onto it.

The day after the ceremony, everyone gathered again. An afterparty. I almost didn't go. But something inside me felt lighter than it had in months. Like a weight I hadn't even realized I was carrying had finally been set down. My chest felt open. My breathing slowed. For the first time in three months, my nervous system wasn't screaming. I could breathe. I laughed. I talked. I stood in the sun without scanning for danger. My friend, the one who had guided me toward the ceremony in the first place, stood beside me. We took a picture together. Nothing dramatic. Just proof of being alive. Of surviving something. Proof of what just happened. I posted it. Up until that moment, Lucy had watched everything. Every story. Every post. Every version of me unraveling in real time. That picture was the last thing she ever watched. The moment she saw it, she unfollowed me. No message. No warning. No goodbye. Just gone. It felt like watching a candle finally go out after months of flickering. When I came home a few days later, the calm didn't last. The silence was louder than anything I'd experienced before. The watching was gone. She had been gone for months already, but the watching had been my illusion. My proof. My thread, it was still alive. Without it, panic rushed in. So I called her. I didn't expect her to answer. I almost hoped she wouldn't. When her name lit up my phone, my heart slammed so hard it made me dizzy. She had ignored me for three months. Ignored the novels I wrote her. The five-minute voice messages. The endless apologies. Every attempt to explain myself. To save us. She answered as if I were a stranger. "Can I help you?" Flat. Cold. Annoyed. I asked if we could talk. She sighed. "We already talked. We broke up. We had this conversation." My mind froze. When? The last time I'd seen her, I had handed her money for her car. She hugged me awkwardly. Like, she barely recognized me. Then she vanished. That was the end. "I don't fuck with you," she said. She repeated it. Again. And again. Eight times. I asked what I had done. "You deserve everything I've done to you," she said. "And more." My hands were shaking now. I asked her to explain. She brought up Disneyland. The trip that was supposed to mean everything. The moment that cracked something we never repaired, but never happened. I suddenly realized I was being punished for choosing my children over her. I tried to tell her I loved her. That I cared about her. That none of this was intentional. She cut me off. "I might have loved you at first," she said, "until I realized what kind of person you are." "What kind of person am I?" I asked. "You're attention seeking," she said. "You'll post literally anything for attention. There's no limit." I stared at the wall, the words ringing in my ears. Because everything I posted had been for her. Her attention. Her presence. Her face at the top of my screen. I didn't care about anyone else. I never did. I kept talking. Desperate now. I thought if she understood how bad I was doing, she might soften. Might finally see me. Might care. I told her how close I'd come to ending everything before that trip. Then she told me I needed psychiatric help. Mocked the ceremony, calling it a "Mushroom trip." Reduced everything I'd gone through to something small. Something stupid. When I tried to explain again how close I had come to killing myself, her voice snapped. "Don't even do that," she said. "You know how he died. How fucking dare you say that to me?" The words hit like a slap. "Don't ever talk to me again." The line went dead. I sat there holding my phone, listening to the silence where her voice had been. That was it. Three months of watching. Of hoping. Of constructing entire worlds around a single notification. Gone in one call. The pressure I had been holding finally gave way. Something inside me blew apart. Just a quiet, devastating rupture. The kind that changes you forever. I never heard her voice again.

20

BECKY THE BITTER END

For the next few months, I ignored every woman who tried to talk to me. Mere distractions from healing. I had always had a following online. Social media full of faces. Messages. Attention that never really meant anything. A constant

background noise of interest that I barely registered anymore. And then there was Becky. I don't know why it was her. I don't know what separated her from everyone else. I just know that the first time I saw her, something in me leaned forward. She wasn't just beautiful. She felt real. Unpolished. Unapologetically herself.

Even with a million girls watching me, I wanted her attention. Just hers. This was the first time I had felt anything internally since Lucy. Becky had dark hair and striking features. The kind that made people look twice without knowing why. There was something unmistakably Latin about her, a kind of grounded sensuality, like she belonged to rhythm before she belonged to conversation. Music wasn't just something she liked. It lived in her. It showed in the way she moved, the way she talked. She was beautiful in a way that demanded attention. Everywhere she went, heads turned. Men noticed her immediately, instinctively, like it wasn't even a choice. She wore big red lipstick like armor, like a signature, like she knew exactly what it did and didn't feel the need to apologize for it. Her body was flawless, the kind of body guys fantasize about, the kind that looks unreal until it's standing right in front of you. She carried it effortlessly, as it had never once been a question whether she was desirable. She knew she was. She didn't flirt for validation. She deflected attention because there was too much of it. Men hovered. Lingering looks. Conversations that tried too hard. She brushed them off so often it became second nature, like swatting away something annoying rather than tempting. Being wanted wasn't special to her. It was constant. When she smiled at me, it felt like luck. Like I'd somehow slipped past the crowd and landed somewhere I wasn't supposed to be. I mistook that feeling for connection. I always did. The longer I talked to her, the more familiar it felt. Not because Becky wasn't unique, she was, but because the way I loved her was already mapped inside me. The way I pictured her walking into rooms. The way I measured myself by her attention. The way her beauty felt like proof that I was enough, that I was chosen, that I mattered. And that's when it hit me.

Lucy had been pale and sharp, quiet and precise. Becky was cold but vivid, loud in all the right ways. Different hair. Different energy. Different music playing in the background. But the feeling was identical. The gravity. The obsession. The way my nervous system locked onto both of them like they were oxygen. I wasn't falling in love with the woman. I was reenacting something. Different faces. Same hunger. Different bodies. Same ache. I kept reaching for beauty the way I always had, as if I could just hold it long enough, it would finally make me whole. But standing there with Becky, feeling that familiar pull, I realized I wasn't chasing love. I was repeating myself. As we started talking. Same thing that always happens, same pattern. Talk a lot, get super close, then disappear. Exactly like Lucy. Months would pass. No warning. No explanation. Just absence. And then, out of nowhere, she would reappear like nothing had happened. Same voice. Same warmth. Same intensity. Each time she came back, it felt closer. Deeper. More intimate. And the strangest part was that we had never met. Months went by like that. Entire seasons. Strictly online. Words on a screen. Phone calls, then disappearance. Her voice telling me pieces of her life, her trauma, her pain. Things she didn't tell other people. I recognized it immediately. She was broken in the same way I was. And I was drawn to it the way I always am. Her darkness didn't scare me. It felt familiar. Comfortable. Like something I knew how to hold. I wanted to fix her. I wanted to be the one who stayed. That was my pattern. Every time. A different face, the same role. When she disappeared, it wasn't cruelty. It was trauma. Every time we got close, it triggered something in her. She would open up, pour everything out, and then vanish. Weeks without a word. No goodbye. No fight. Just gone. And I let it happen. Over and over. We both loved music. The emo kind that screamed the way we would scream inside. The kind that made us feel alive when nothing else could. The kind that makes us not feel the pain, at least for a second. I planned my first trip to Vans Warped Tour in Florida, and she was the first person I thought of. "I wish you could come," I told her. "I'll buy you a ticket." She couldn't get the time off work. So I went alone. But even there, surrounded by noise and heat and crowds, I was thinking about her. Walking the grounds, scanning tables, booths, and merch tents. She collected records, but not casually. She cared about the art. The story. The special editions. The meaning behind the object. So I searched. I didn't want something generic. I wanted something that felt like her. Something rare. Something intentional. Something that said I see you without needing explanation. I found it. A special edition from one of her favorite bands. Before that, she had asked me to send her flowers. So I did. Later, she told me another guy had been there when they arrived. He had walked outside, seen the flowers, and it had been awkward. She said it lightly. Like it didn't matter. But it lodged itself in my chest anyway. When

I got back from Florida, I mailed her the record. I already had her address from the flowers. When she received it, she lit up. Messages poured in. Gratitude. Emotion. Telling me how much it meant to her. How special it was. And for a moment, it felt like I had done something right. Then she disappeared again. Black Friday came. Warped Tour tickets for the following year went on sale. I didn't want to go alone again. I didn't want to stand in a crowd, feeling detached from my own life alone. I wanted to experience it with someone who would actually feel it the way I did. So I bought her a ticket. I told her. She didn't react with excitement. "What?" she said. "Why would you do that?" Then she said, "Don't worry. You'll find someone better to go with by then." "No," I said. "You're going with me." She pulled back once again. The whiplash from it all was unbearable. Weeks passed. Then she came back again. She lived about an hour and fifteen minutes away. Eventually, we met. In real life. When I walked into her house, it felt surreal. Like stepping into a place I'd already been in my dreams. She was exactly who I imagined. When we sat and talked, it felt like slipping into something familiar and dangerous at the same time. She felt like home, like Lucy, or at least how I hope she would feel if she ever came back. She felt like home, or what I thought home was supposed to feel like. I don't know if it was real or something I projected onto her. I still don't. When it was time to leave, she said, "Well... I guess this is it." I nodded. "Yeah. I guess this is the final season." She smiled, half-serious. "If this is the finale," she said, "maybe it should end more intimately." I asked for a hug. We hugged. Then I kissed her. Then we didn't stop. It just kept going and going until I was in her bed. When I touched her, when I held her, something inside me unlocked. It wasn't just desire. It was recognition. Like touching a wound that already knew me. Like holding someone whose pain matched mine perfectly. The night ended with orgasms, loud ones that shook her whole house. I thought the neighbors were going to call the cops with how loud her screams were. I walked out of there with deep scratches all over my chest and back afterward. In the coming weeks, everything in me panicked. The fear of abandonment surged all at once. The terror of losing that feeling. Of losing her. Of losing home. I didn't let things settle. I didn't give it space. To let it breathe. I tried harder. Too hard. On Christmas Day, I sent her another record. Another special edition. One of five hundred. I bought it on eBay so it would surprise her. When it arrived, she got scared. She thought someone had found her address. A seller from eBay mailed it to her. She didn't even ask if it was me. I had to find out the misunderstanding from a story on her socials. It was me. I told her. She didn't seem to care. Then I escalated again. She didn't want to make the 12-hour drive to Long Beach, so I bought plane tickets for us. I sent her a long message explaining it around Christmas, trying to make it sound thoughtful instead of desperate. Trying to make it sound like love instead of fear. And then she disappeared. Didn't even acknowledge any of it. So I got in my feelings and posted too much, said too much, tried to catch her attention too hard. A few days later, she blocked me. Everywhere. On literally every platform. No explanation. No conversation. No ending. Just silence. And the worst part wasn't losing her. It was realizing I had felt the ending coming the entire time. Like my body knew how this story ended before my heart ever caught up. When I realized she had blocked me on everything, my body didn't react as a normal person's would. There was no gradual sadness. No slow understanding. It was like a bomb went off inside me. All at once. Every abandonment I had ever survived collapsed into a single moment. Every person I had ever loved. Every parent. Every family member. Every goodbye I never got. Lucy. All came back at the same time, stacked on top of each other, crushing down in one violent wave. It wasn't just her. It felt like everyone disappeared again. My chest locked up. The pain wasn't emotional in some abstract way. It was physical. Heavy. Pressurized. Like something was squeezing my heart so hard it might actually stop. I remember thinking I couldn't breathe, but I was breathing. I remember sitting there feeling like I had been hollowed out from the inside. That's what PTSD feels like. Not fear. Not panic. Reliving loss as if it's happening again. My nervous system didn't know this was one person blocking me online. It thought I was a kid again. Thought everyone was gone. Thought I had been left behind permanently. Felt the world had proven, one more time, that nothing stays. I didn't sleep much. Time blurred. And then, slowly, I came back. It didn't happen all at once. It never does. The pain loosened its grip little by little. My body remembered how to exist again. How to breathe without bracing. How to sit in a room without feeling like it was collapsing inward. Life moved forward. I moved forward. But here's the part that never left. I still dreamt about her. Not every night. Not constantly. But enough. Enough that it mattered. She showed up the same way every time. Familiar. Warm. Close. Like nothing ever ended. Like the distance never existed. Like I finally get to stay in the moment my body thought it found home. Then I wake up. And the feeling is gone again. Some people don't haunt you because they were perfect. They haunt you because they touched a wound that was already there. And you never forgot what it felt like to almost believe you were home. Life doesn't end the way movies promise it will. There is no final explosion. No slow-motion victory. No moment where everything finally makes sense. It just gets quieter. In my early twenties, I mistook noise for living. Parties. Girls. Movement for the sake of movement. I thought if I kept running, nothing could catch me. In my mid-twenties and thirties, the world narrowed. Not because it got smaller, but because it became clearer. Everything I was became about two small people who didn't ask to be here and trusted me anyway. I built my life around protecting them. Feeding them. Showing up even when I was empty. Giving them what I never had. That became the mission. That became the meaning. And then something strange happens when you do that long enough. They grow. Quietly. Gradually. Without asking your permission. One day, you realize they don't need you the same way anymore. The hands-on part fades. The emergencies slow down. The dependency loosens its grip. You're still their father. That never leaves. But the role shifts. You move from center stage to the sidelines. Watching. Hoping you did enough when it mattered most. Trusting that the love you poured in stays put even when you step back. That transition is its own kind of grief. No one warns you about it. After decades of being needed, the silence can feel like a void if you're not careful. I look back on the last twenty years and see chapters defined by survival. By chaos. By becoming whatever was required to keep going. I ask myself what the next decade is for. What a man in his forties is supposed to build when the urgency fades. Marriage never felt like a promise waiting for me. More like a door that was already closed. Or maybe one that was never mine to open. And for a long time, I thought that meant something was missing. That I had failed some invisible test. But now I'm not so sure. Maybe purpose isn't about chasing anymore. Maybe it's about steadiness. About becoming someone your children remember as solid. Present. Unshakeable. A man who didn't disappear when things got hard. A man who chose peace after a lifetime of chaos. Not because he was tired, but because he was done running. I've spent my life learning how to survive. Now I'm learning how to stay. There are still scars. There are still ghosts. They don't vanish just because the noise stops. But they don't drive the story anymore. They sit quietly in the background, reminders of where I've been and what I endured. Proof that I lived through something instead of being erased by it. Some people are shaped by destruction. Others learn to build with what's left. This is not a redemption story. It's a continuation. I'm still here. Still standing. Still choosing. And for the first time, that feels like enough.

Now I know.

And that knowledge doesn't save

There was never a word for me.

Not growing up. Not while everything was happening. Not while I was being punished for things I couldn't explain, hated for things I didn't understand, and praised for things that were slowly killing me.

People called me intense. Difficult. Too much. Too sensitive. Too quiet. Too loud. Too honest. Too strange. Too obsessive. Too detached. Too emotional. Too cold.

Every contradiction at once.

I learned early that whatever I was, it was wrong.

So I learned to perform around it.

I learned how to mirror people so they wouldn't notice how little sense the world made to me. I studied tone, timing, posture, and jokes. I memorized reactions the way other kids memorized math. I learned when to smile. When to shut up. When to disappear. When to become whoever would be tolerated in that room.

What nobody ever saw was the cost.

The exhaustion of pretending not to hear lights buzzing. The way sound hit me was like an impact. How certain fabrics felt unbearable against my skin. How eye contact felt invasive, like standing under a spotlight I didn't ask for. How rules mattered more to me than people because rules didn't shift without warning.

They didn't see the panic when plans changed. The way my body locked up when expectations weren't clear. The way my mind latched onto patterns, details, and obsessions and refused to let go. How I could feel everything and nothing at the same time.

They saw defiance.

They saw arrogance.

They saw apathy.

They saw a kid who didn't listen.

They didn't see a nervous system permanently braced for impact.

They didn't see how literal I was. How words landed inside me exactly as spoken. How sarcasm confused me. How cruelty disguised as humor carved deep, permanent grooves into my sense of self.

They didn't see that when I withdrew, it wasn't indifference. It was overload.

They didn't see that when I exploded, it wasn't anger. It was collapse.

So I kept collecting evidence that I was broken.

That something in me was defective. That I was missing whatever everyone else had received naturally. I watched people move through life effortlessly, reading rooms I couldn't decode, navigating hierarchies I couldn't see, breaking rules without consequence, while I was punished for breathing wrong.

I blamed myself for everything.

The bullying. The isolation. The way relationships imploded. The way I loved too hard or not at all. The way substances quieted my brain in ways nothing else ever had. The way chaos felt familiar and calm felt suspicious.

I thought I was dangerous.

I thought I was unlovable.

I thought I was fundamentally wrong.

And then, much later, after the damage had already stacked up, after entire versions of myself had been burned down just to survive, someone finally said the word no one had ever said to me before.

Level 1 Autism Spectrum Disorder.

Not as an excuse. Not as a diagnosis meant to shrink me. As an explanation.

Suddenly, the entire map rearranged itself.

The childhood sensory overload. The hyperfixations. The rigid morality. The inability to tolerate hypocrisy. The black-and-white thinking that made me uncompromising. The deep empathy that broke my chest open and the shutdowns that followed. The social exhaustion. The masking. The burnout. The way I could be brilliant in isolation and lost in groups.

It wasn't moral failure.

It wasn't defiance.

It wasn't weakness.

It was a nervous system wired differently in a world that punishes difference.

I wasn't broken.

I was unsupported.

I wasn't dangerous.

I was overwhelmed.

I wasn't cold.

I was protecting myself the only way I knew how.

That realization didn't erase what happened to me. It didn't soften the trauma or excuse the harm. It didn't turn pain into something noble.

But it did something more important.

It told the truth.

For the first time, my entire life stopped feeling like a series of unrelated disasters and started feeling like a single, coherent story. One where a child with an unrecognized disorder. Who was raised in chaos, punished for symptoms, groomed for compliance, then blamed for the damage that followed.

A story where survival required shapeshifting.

Where love was conditional.

Where safety was inconsistent.

Where being misunderstood wasn't an accident. It was the baseline.

I am not writing this for pity.

I am writing this for clarity.

Because once you understand this, everything else makes sense. The obsession. The intensity. The isolation. The self-destruction. The relentless drive. The inability to half feel anything. The way I could endure what should have broken me and still collapse over things others found trivial.

This book was never about being reckless.

It was about being misread.

It was never about excess.

It was about regulation.

It was never about chaos.

It was about a nervous system trying to survive in a world that never slowed down enough to see it.

I spent a lifetime being told who I was by people who never bothered to understand how I was built.

Now I know.

And that knowledge doesn't save me.

It frees me.

Because for the first time, the story doesn't end with shame.

It ends with truth.

EPILOGUE

NOTHING LEFT

It was late. Just dark enough to feel empty. I pulled into the Fred Meyer parking lot straight from work, and then I saw it.

That car.

Same color. Same shape. Same stupid, familiar outline. The kind of car that had trained my nervous system without my permission. My brain did the same thing it had done a thousand times before over the last year—filled with hope that it was her, then disappointment. Over and over. Always the same result.

It was never her.

I almost laughed to myself. There it was. Lucy's car. Or at least the ghost of it. I had seen versions of it everywhere—in parking lots, at stoplights, on side streets—and it always triggered the same flicker in my chest.

But this time, it wasn't wrong.

I pulled in closer and realized the car wasn't empty. The interior light was on. She was sitting there, right in front of me, wearing her big black glasses. Her head was tilted down, her beautiful face illuminated by the glowing phone screen in her hands. Alone. Late. Still.

It took a second for my brain to catch up, like reality was buffering. This couldn't be real, but it was. There she was. Not a memory. Not a lookalike. Not a trick of pattern recognition. Lucy. The real her. Solid, not a dream. Sitting in her car like I had imagined so many times.

I parked two cars away.

I couldn't stop looking. I didn't want to be seen, so I just watched. She never looked up, and I found myself asking questions I had no right to ask anymore. Why was she sitting here this late? Was she waiting for someone? A boyfriend? Why was she here? Was she okay?

A year had passed since I'd last seen her. A year full of things I would never know about. New mornings. New damage. New versions of herself I had never met. I wondered what happened to her during that time. If she was happier. If she was safe. If life had been kinder to her than I had been to myself.

I went into the store. Wandered the aisles without purpose. Twenty minutes passed, and when I came back out, I hoped she was gone.

She wasn't.

Same position. Same glow. Same stillness.

I walked past her car, close enough to feel the weight of it. She didn't see me. Not then. I got into my car, hands on the wheel, knuckles white. My heart was beating so fast I couldn't breathe. I felt like I was going to pass out.

As I pulled forward, passing her window, she suddenly jerked her head up and looked right at me. I don't know if she saw my car. Or my face. Or if she felt someone staring at her. Our eyes didn't meet. Or maybe they almost did. I will never be sure.

And then I drove away.

Just like that.

No wave. No reunion. No closure scene. No music. Just two people orbiting the same parking lot for a moment, completely unknown to each other.

It struck me then how strange it was. How someone whose heartbeat I once knew against my chest, how someone I fell in love with one beat at a time, could become a stranger I walked past in the dark. How easily a whole history could collapse into a passing glance, as if it never even happened.

I didn't feel pain exactly. I just missed the version of her that used to be mine.

Was she okay? Was she happy? I hoped so.

Then the light changed, the parking lot disappeared behind me, and she went back to being a person I used to know.

I didn't know where I was going. I just kept driving for over an hour.

Then suddenly, I did.

I turned down the same driveway that still felt like Micky and Kevin. The house was dark and empty, filled with the ghosts of a past life.

I came back not to remember, not to heal, but because I had run out of places to run.

This house had held everything before I knew how to destroy it.

I walked inside alone. Nothing had changed, yet everything had. The rooms were empty but not quiet. Ghosts moved through them. Not the scary kind; the ordinary kind. There was laughter in places where no one stood, arguments without voices, and kids running through hallways that hadn't felt small enough for them in years.

I saw versions of myself I didn't recognize. I saw versions of myself I did.

I had lived a whole life trying to escape this place. Trying to outrun grief. Responsibility. The version of me that started here—before the noise, before the chaos, before the damage.

I never realized I was circling the same point the entire time.

Everything I had become was just distance. Everything I had lost was just proof. I had to live an entire life to end up exactly where I'd started.

As I walked up to the old family fireplace, I imagined everyone alive. All that was left was a single family photo sitting there, cracked and withered by time. It had been sitting there, abandoned, for years.

I made a fire. It was small, but enough to light the dark house like a candle in a cavern. Then I threw the picture in and watched it burn.

I never said my name before because I didn't know who I was. Not really. Not until this moment.

I am Blake Jerome Humphreys.

ACKNOWLEDGMENTS

I WOULD LIKE TO thank my friend Ryan for never giving up and never walking away, for being a friend, a best friend, and a brother. You were the one person who never gave up on me.

To my children, thank you for being the reason I get up every morning and keep fighting. Everything I do, I do for you.

And to every woman mentioned in this book, thank you for the lessons, the heartbreak, and the clarity. You did not just break me. You exposed every weak foundation I was still standing on. Because of you, I rebuilt myself brick by brick, without illusions, without excuses, and without needing anyone to save me. I do not regret any of it. What rose from the ashes will never break again.

Even when everyone else gives up on you, never give up on yourself.

ABOUT THE AUTHOR

BLAKE JEROME HUMPHREYS DOES not write safe stories. He writes what breaks. He grew up around the shine of Hollywood and saw early how illusion can look like identity. That fracture between image and truth became the core of his voice. His work lives in the tension between ego and collapse, power and consequence, who we pretend to be and who we are when everything is stripped away. For over a decade in healthcare, Blake has stood in rooms where seconds matter. He has watched life leave a body. He has fought to keep it there. He has seen families fall apart and strangers hold hands in their final moments. Those experiences did not make him numb. They made him aware. They made him grateful. They made him understand how thin the line is between now and never. That is why he writes the way he does. Not to shock. Not to perform. But because life is fragile and truth should not be watered down. His voice is raw, reflective, and grounded in lived experience. Darkness is present, but so is grace. When he is not writing, he is studying human behavior and raising his sons, who remind him daily that real strength is quiet, earned, and proven when no one is watching.